# LIFE UNSPOKEN

### THE MORE YOU SHARE, THE CLOSER YOU COME TO TRUE RELATIONSHIPS

## GREGORY B. DAVIS

Life Unspoken - The more you share, the closer you come to true relationships

Heart artwork design by **Georgina Frias** (back cover).

ISBN 978-1-7348643-4-2 (ebook)

ISBN 978-1-7348643-5-9 (print)

Thank you to my family. Always.

## GREGORY B. DAVIS
A NOTE FROM THE AUTHOR

Today — looking back and thinking about numerous interactions and conversations when I chose silence because I was fearful of making a mistake or of vulnerability — I feel grateful to know that life is better when we share it. With my many years of experience in the Personal Growth area, my research and work with people, I've come to write this, my third book: Life Unspoken.

I believe that our lives need to be spoken about in depth and deserve to be shared with our loved ones. Unfortunately, after years of observation, I've found that it is a challenge for most individuals to open up. Sadly, this robs us of meaningful knowledge, wisdom and most importantly, the connection we long for in our lives.

Understanding that it is not easy, I applaud you for picking up this book and for working your way to a fuller life.

# CONTENTS

# INTRODUCTION

When you think about your life and analyze the things that really matter to you —the ones that move you forward, and keep you feeling loved and alive— those are, without a doubt, your meaningful relationships.

You encounter love and meaning when you connect with others in a deep manner, by choosing to be vulnerable. It is important to note that what you verbally and emotionally put into each relationship is what you'll receive in return; the amount you are open, and allow others to see your inner self, will lead to the amount others will be open with you. Because only when you embrace community will community embrace you, and at this point you will experience connection and belonging.

Part of what I do for a living is present a family and teen program called *Choices Teen and Family Camp*. I have learned, over and over again, that our closest relationships are the center of our well-being as humans. Therefore, how would your life be different if you were fully thriving in your relationships?

The teen and family summer program normally receives approximately 35 families who work on their growth as a family as a whole; it starts with the personal growth of the children and then as a family unit — noting that parents had previously worked on their own personal betterment before working on their relationship with their kids. The goal of this program is to improve that relationship, taking it to the next more-loving level. During one of the summers, I witnessed an interaction that has forever changed the way I feel and think about the presence of silence in my life, and today I would like to share it with you:

For this specific memory and exercise, I was in front of the room filled with approximately 120 individuals (parents and children), and I was taken aback by the power and insight of one child.

The activity we were working on required each family to come to the front of the room and respond to a series of questions. The children, with whom we had been working with and preparing for this interaction over the prior few days, were given the first turn.
We started with this question: "What is one thing the parent could do something about to improve the relationship?"

The child standing in front of the parent said: "Don't lie to me and stay in silence about your life."

The parent was surprised to hear this and took a minute, trying to understand where the child was coming from with such a comment. Then the parent, with complete focus and attention on the child, responded: "I do not lie to you, I'm very open with you about my life. What is the reason you'd ask that from me?"

The child quickly said: "When you get home every evening and I ask how your day went, you always respond "fine" then you go into your room in silence... and I know that doesn't mean fine. You are not fine."

In the moment of the interchange, the parent was emotionally disconcerted, but stated they were accountable for the distance that the habit of silence had created. Furthermore, they acknowledged the lack of words was not a healthy form of communication for their relationship.

I made a point to seek out the parent at a later date and obtain their perspective of silence in the relationship. They spoke of the clarity which had been obtained, that in truth there were no secrets (even between parent and child). Life was rough at times but the choice of silence was not protecting the child, and the parent was determined to find a

way to speak about difficult topics in an appropriate manner.

It took me quite a few days to completely wrap my
head around this profound family moment. The
interaction kept reappearing in my thoughts
when I had a moment of idleness. What I learned
is that one of the most significant causes of
distance in relationships is silence.

I am a son, a husband, a father, a brother, a friend.
Since that family camp, I have incorporated the lessons
from this story for myself and all the relationships in my
life. My relationships improve and deepen when I speak
about topics that matter with my loved ones. My relationships suffer, on every occasion, when I go silent.

Wildly interesting is that when an individual (or individuals) makes a habit of turning to the game of silence
in their relationships, the internal voices within both
parties are **anything but silent.** When this environment
is created—in any type of relationship— there is lack of
information, expression and conversation on both sides.
All individuals turn inwards, further empowering their
limiting internal voices, like **a dark place tucked away** in
their thoughts. Next, unfortunately, begins a lot of mind
reading, when one or both individuals in the relationship
attempts to discern what their partner is thinking,
believing and/or feeling. What they are left with is the
hurtful questioning about the other's commitment to the
relationship, space, **and continued silence between
them.** In many cases, the relationship has no chance to

grow, learn, or even reach a common ground as the individual is static with only themself to take the relationship somewhere, somehow.

Therefore, I ask you: Does **silence in your relationships** make you happy? No. It is **love** that makes you happy. It is **connection** that keeps you in a good place. It is belonging... and it all starts with **you saying what is important to you and electing to engage in profound conversation.**

I acknowledge that opening can be a frightening endeavor, and this very fear can set up decisions that impact our entire lives and relationships. We all have faced rejection and disappointment at some point in our life, and when our moment of vulnerability was rejected or not returned, it hurt. In a way, it might seem safer to keep quiet and closed off, versus being open to others.

Short-term versus long-term impact of secrets in a relationship have conflicting and decidedly negative outcomes. While in the short term, **unspoken words** have the desired brief effect of making you feel safe. Unfortunately, in the moment it is difficult to discern the true cost to the relationship.

Over the long term, secrets lead to more secrets and the subsequent lack of ability to **understand what should be kept to oneself, and what is healing to say.** Added up, over the short and long term, all of these factors (secrets, silence, and loneliness) are impacting the health of your relationship in a dramatic manner.

Today, right at this moment, the silence in your life might be defining your closest relationships and expanding your loneliness. All this in the belief that you're creating a perceived self-preservation, but the truth is that people in your life see it and feel it.

So, I would like you to ask yourself this: What do I want out of my life? Am I happy with my current relationships? Am I fulfilled, living at peace and experiencing belonging to my community?

To me, it seems worth reconsidering your choice of silence. In this book, together we will examine how and why silence is used in our relationships; we will see the value and benefits of sharing secrets, unveil the reasons to open up, and learn the steps that will bring us healing.

Shall we begin?

## THE RIDE

OPENING STORY

The first two hours were pleasant, the second two hours were a challenge, but I enjoyed the physical push and touch of exhaustion but the final two hours pedalling on that road bike were neither pleasant nor enjoyable... what had I gotten myself into? I'd signed up to be on a team of six to ride relay style (24 hours a day) with five other teams from Calgary, Canada, to San Jose, California.

I chose this trial because of two big life events which had taken place in a five month period. First, I'd been diagnosed with cancer and had three surgeries and three rounds of extremely potent chemotherapy. Second, I'd lost one of my best friends to the same disease. My physical traumas were healing swiftly, the scars were mending, my hair was regrowing, my weight was returning. However, my mental state was showing little betterment. Specifically, when my friend came to mind, I was still overcome with emotion (no doubt my own traumas intertwined with the pain of him passing). The bottom line is that I missed him and could not understand the reason he was taken from this world. My first instinct, and reaction, was to move to a place of **silence**. I was so unsure how to proceed that I focused on my life again, I stuffed my feelings down and kept the **secrets** of my pain locked up. I thought things would go back to the way they'd always been — normal.

I know now in that moment of wanting normalcy I'd decided that silence was the best way forward. There was some return to my ordinary life, however there was a part of me that kept looking back... my mind would spin with what I should have said or done. As the days, weeks, and months passed, I moved to avoid interaction and specific topics if I believed it would lead me back to the pain in some manner.

I found, over time, the longer I sat in silence the louder my internal voice grew and the more distance I felt from the loved ones in my family, friends and community. I felt alone with loved ones all around me. As the year passed, the act of silence and keeping my feelings a secret, I'd determined that my actions had not helped my situation and feeling towards my emotional challenges. I understood on some level, I needed **to do something different** and take steps to heal.

What I acknowledge today is that secrets and silence had robbed me of being purely authentic, that I'd missed opportunities to heal and grow and this had put a wedge in my key relationships. All of this I knew in my logical head, having worked in personal growth, but I lacked the clarity to put curative actions into my life. I'd by-passed many occasions to be open and honest with myself and others which would have given me more self-confidence and shared empowerment with others. I know now that there is no one more powerful than the individual who lives in pure vulnerability. It says to the world, this is who I am, these are the challenges I overcame, these are the mistakes I made and all of them make me better today.

I knew I needed to take a step towards healing. I was not sure of the exact direction or point but I knew forgiveness was likely the most healthy starting point for me instead of silence and regarding the passing of my friend. I read, journalled and attended a men's weekend retreat which brought a step of peace to my life. Balance was returning, I could feel myself becoming more healthy.

I did have a realization about forgiveness -- it is never finished. Something would catch me off-guard, I'd have a dream, a memory would reappear and I was jerked right back into the past. I'd start my forgiveness work again to find equilibrium, however I could just as easily move from balance to pain and more silence at a moment's notice.

I found that this emotional see-saw only compounded the challenging situation and drove me to a place of feeling lonely. I needed a next step, one that along with forgiveness would lead me to not only feel empowered but also open to express the entirety of the challenges that cancer and the loss had brought to my life the year before.

Only when I learned the deepest truth, of the ideals of Create Value, did true long term healing take place. That truth is that I not only needed forgiveness in my life but also a manner in which to Create Value and bring abundance to myself and others. This combination for me meant that at last I would be free from the weight of past painful memories. Secrets and silence took away what I wanted to feel and have in life and they were and still are part of the forgiveness and creation of value process.

In summary, we all have pain in our past and it impacts our lives today. Silence is not your friend, it provides no healing nor growth. Secrets cause you to move to silence and keep you locked in the past. Both of which create an environment of feeling lonely and alone. The healthiest steps possible are opening up and talking about the past. This allows you to bring the wound out to the open to heal. Then the gift of forgiveness can start and foster more balance and healing in life. Finally, the most powerful step of all which goes hand in hand with forgiveness, creating value out of the painful past will create more power, joy, openness, wisdom and connection.

# SILENCE
## THREE STATES

S ilence is a fascinating state of being to consider. It can be used in many situations — some healthy, some not. It can be used to honor what someone is saying or to show immense disagreement. It can give you time to think and formulate your best response or it can act as an insurmountable emotional wall. Too often we think silence will keep us safe or create a safe place. In reality it is used as the ultimate "gotcha" in relationships all too often. Let's take a deeper look at differing types of silence for our purposes.

There are three types of silence for the function of our book:

Peaceful
Punishing
Protective

First, we will touch upon **Peaceful Silence**. It is **not** the scope of this book and is an important part of a healthy state of mind. Peaceful silence is a state of comfortable quiet perhaps with a touch of mental curiosity. This type of silence can be held alone or in the presence of a trusted companion. There are many times in which a peaceful silence can be sought in life — when contemplating a challenge, looking for a key piece of information, or simply to find what there is to find. There are seminars and retreats which focus on silence, those can be incredibly enlightening. Peaceful silence is calming internally and externally and completely healthy.

Next we look at **Punishing Silence**. This is not a healthy state of quiet and silence. Punishing Silence is commonly found in long-term relationships, especially relationships that have experienced deep hurt and/or one where it was a learned manner to fight with a partner. It is commonly referred to as the "Silent Treatment" and in my opinion is an ugly way to engage (or disengage) during moments of conflict.

Typically punishing silence leads to more punishing silence and often both partners use it to get back at the other, leading to immense walls that grow thicker and higher as the years pass.

If you are an expert in the silent treatment, there is very little a loved one can do to engage you in dialogue. In my experience this is the ultimate controlling mechanism, one of the ultimate fighting weapons.

Finally, our last form of silence is **Protective**, which is used to protect yourself from anything and anyone in life. On some levels, and many levels, you believe that you are protecting yourself by hiding and not speaking. Risking a deep conversation which might lead to a sensitive area is to be avoided at all costs. This creates distance in all relationships, and in oneself, plus it leaves those around you wondering the reason for the perceived distance.

We will look more deeply at **Punishing and Protective Silence** in the coming chapters. These two types of silence resemble an environment of gentle and comfort, however it can be just the opposite, as we will explore, even violent.

# LONELINESS

Loneliness is not a common topic of discussion in a social setting; it is the antithesis of a meeting between friends, family or loved ones. The topic of loneliness can be an unsettling word, state, feeling of which no one wants to be involved. It carries a negative stigma in society that if someone is lonely, there is an issue with the core of who they are and it might be contagious in some manner.

Conversely, we've all experienced the feeling of loneliness at times in our life and have had to find our way out. For reasons we'll explore in this book, some find their way out and unfortunately some do not. Loneliness can be in a moment, long term or an entire lifetime. It can lead to health issues or move individuals to action to make a change. It is becoming an enormous issue for our society and not only does it impact our psyche, but it also directly impacts our physical health.

What is loneliness? For starters it is to feel a lack of

social connection. It can show up in the quality (or lack of quality) of a relationship and how vulnerable you can be! Words used to describe the lonely state are: empty, sad, alone and unwanted. It can morph into many different reactions: anger, irritability, hostility, shyness, anxiety, awkwardness and low self-esteem, etc... It may also be a combination of the list and cycle through numerous emotional states.

According to the article "The Structure and Spread of Loneliness in a Large Social Network" by Cacioppo, Fowler and Christakis, there are unfortunate aspects of loneliness which people will experience such as; "they tend to be shyer, more anxious, more hostile, more socially awkward and lower in self esteem."[1] The authors continue; "...when people feel lonely they tend to act toward others in a less trusting and more hostile fashion."[2]

It has become such an issue in the Western world that Britain has appointed a "Minister of Loneliness."[3] Theresa May, former Prime Minister of the UK said, "Loneliness is one of the greatest public health challenges..." In the aforementioned article, it states that three quarters of those surveyed felt loneliness, which is linked to health impacts such as heart disease, stroke and Alzheimer's disease. Finally and almost unbelievably, the article states, "around 200,000 older people have not had a conversation with a friend or relative in more than a month."[4]

To take the physical health impact a step deeper former Surgeon General Dr Vivek Murthy has spoken and written regularly that loneliness is an epidemic and can be fatal. One of Dr. Vivek's more impactful quotes is "Loneliness and weak social connections are associated with a reduction in lifespan similar to that caused by smoking 15 cigarettes a day and even greater than that associated with obesity."[5] Loneliness is solely about lack of conversations, interactions and friendship. It goes beyond and impacts us in many manners which are more profound.

What is the root cause of loneliness and its impact on society? There are a number of factors that have, over decades, eroded our societies, communities, friendships and families. Some of the factors that have increased decreased social interaction are more people living alone, less dense living environments, and technology. Each of these factors have led to a slow and steady lessening of contact and sense of community. According to the U.S. Census Bureau, the percentage of single person dwellings since 1940 to 2000 has increased from 7.7 percent in the 1940s to 28.4 percent in 2019!

Additionally, for renters (not including single family owned homes) the rate from 1940 for single individual dwelling was 8% and climbed to 36% in 1980, and in 2018 the rate stood at approximately 43%![6]

While renting versus buying a primary residence and the distance between homes (i.e., population-dense cities versus suburbia) have impacted contact, additional factors which have pushed our self-isolation such as the use of cars versus public transportation, social media, smaller family size, freelance versus permanent work, job availability anywhere in the country and opening to the world, and so on. Each individual factor might not erode our togetherness; however, over time and across many areas of our life, it takes a toll.

Numerous sources and articles are available specifically about loneliness and they all point to the same general conclusion. A few I found are:

"...only around half of Americans say they have meaningful in-person social interactions on a daily basis, such as having an extended conversation with a friend or spending time with family members."[7]

"... a quarter of men have no one outside their immediate family to rely on."[8]

"Nearly half of Americans report sometimes or always feeling alone (46 percent) or left out (47 percent)."[9]

"...research shows about 95% of women both withhold things from loved ones and have lied to someone close to them."[10]

"... one in 10 adults (nine percent) in Japan say they often or always feel lonely..." and "In Japan, more than a third (35 percent) of those who self-identify as lonely say they have felt isolated or lonely for more than 10 years..."[11]

"...25% of respondents say they would often go
days on end without speaking to anyone."[12]

Women, men, young, old, whoever it may be it holds true across almost all spectrums, in today's world we feel solitary and lonely. This leads to having fewer, or no, true confidants on our side when we need to express a difficult situation from the present or past. This leads to almost complete solitude if there's a break in the long-term relationship or divorce. It is a problem in our society and it is only gaining steam.

Here is an example closer to me and my own family, my father tells the following learning from his two uncles (heroes in his mind at a young age) which influenced him greatly growing up. He remembers them telling him, "If you hurt your finger working then stick it in your pocket and don't utter a word. No one wants to hear about your finger." They lived, and my father lived, for many years with this motto, when something bad happened in life "stick it in your pocket and don't say a word." Over a lifetime this leads to fewer opportunities to connect with friends and strengthen relationships.

Upon deeper conversation with my father this story or motto for life from my great uncles, started to connect a key point in the creation of this book as I studied the reasons for loneliness in life. For my father, he took the message as if something bad, hurtful, upsetting, painful happened in his life, he would never turn to a friend, co-worker, mate, counselor, therapist -- never. He would "Stick it in his pocket." This motto encouraged silence vs opening up and thereby causing loneliness. The silence robbed him of the opportunity to be open and create connection with those around him. The guiding light of *Life Unspoken* became clear to me: **Loneliness** in life is created when you choose **Silence** and isolate parts of your past life because you have elected to withhold **Secrets** versus exposing and opening up.

Therefore, at the root of this book lies the truth about your secrets. In this book, you'll see a lot of focus on the three (Loneliness, Silence and Secrets). Secrets are the most difficult to define across a large readership. As you read, take the position that a secret in this book is a broad term. For you a secret might be a deep dark painful memory, for others it might be an upsetting episode with a loved one. It could entail a troubled child or sibling. The point is that you may have not disclosed the painful memory or only revealed it to a small degree.

One other interpretation of the story from my father and how he learned to deal with painful points in his life. Instead of creating and deepening relationships and community in his younger life, he turned to another saying of the key men in his life: "If it isn't working; you are not working hard enough." This phrase operated incredibly well for my father professionally and did not work for him well at home. Thankfully, he finally acknowledged the shortsightedness of the phrase in his life. At that point he re-evaluated his priorities and devoted more time and energy to home. Almost immediately his family relationships improved and continued to strengthen over the years.

Entire books have been written and fields of study have dedicated to feeling alone and the impacts of and from social media. For our consideration, let's take it to the basics of friends and online friends. Which is a more lonely situation; to be 100% authentic, open and vulnerable with friends and they disagree with your opinion and at times can't relate, or be surrounded by 100 coworkers and 1,000 social media "friends" who don't know your simplest truths? I suggest an increasing over-reliance on social media is a short term cover-up for a lack of deep connection **and** robs time and resources from deep relationships. The support received online is fleeting and quickly fades. The darker flip side of support is online chastising, which is quick and can be painful.

While many of the points made in *Life Unspoken* so far have been sad, troublesome and distressing, there is an even darker side to feeling alone. Loneliness, over time, will shorten your life. It will remove years from your life and it is toxic. Those who feel they are shut off are less happy, their health declines earlier in life, their brain function declines sooner, and they live shorter lives plus "...people who are lonely have a greater risk of heart disease, stroke and dementia."[13] This is a serious issue for individuals and society as a whole, and it is completely and joyfully remedied with certain actions, which we will discuss later in the book.

What are the most important things in your life? List five, now narrow that to three items. How many of those are relationships (spouse, friends, co-workers)? Now, think about how you spend your days and weeks. What are the top three items that get a majority of your time? Do the lists match up? Are they even close to what you consider as important aspects for your time? Finally, what do you talk about with this group? Do you discuss things that matter and are important to you, or is it more along the line of small talk about daily activities and complaining? Have you done your part to create a trusting relationship and stepped out of your comfort zone to discuss things that matter?

# THE STUDY

We've established that loneliness is impacting and affecting our society and you from time to time (or maybe all the time). It is a growing reality that, for now, doesn't seem to be lessening. Where can we turn to inform ourselves about what steps to take in order to create better relationships and a better life? I've found the best place to turn is research, and in this case one of the longest running studies from one of the most reputable universities in the world.

Harvard University's Grant and Glueck study was started in 1938 and its goal was to track the physical and emotional welfare then identify predictors of healthy aging. The study focused on two populations: 268 male graduates from Harvard and 456 men living in poverty from Boston's inner city. We will look at the study in more detail. To start us off, consider the words of George Vaillant [1], who lead the research for over 30 years —

> Happiness is love. Full stop.

An overview of the data collected for the study includes:

Data collection through college, questionnaires every 2 years after, psychiatric interviews, institutional records, psychological tests, medical examinations, (social history, intellectual functioning, academic achievement, personality assessment, psychological well being, physiological and medical information, biographical data). Complete physicals were conducted 1969, 1974, 1984, 1989

The results showed that **warm and loving relationships are the key to a happier and healthier life.** There are numerous take-aways from this study; you need people in our life that you can rely on as you make this journey. You must have a community around you to help you deal with hard times. These communities create an outlet that allows you to relax emotionally and physically. This, in turn, keeps your brains and bodies healthier and improves life in all manners. Warm, supportive, close community makes you healthier in every way.

The title of this article out of the Harvard Gazette does the best job of summing up what matters most for our health: "Good genes are nice, but joy is better."[2] In the article there are numerous quotes which perfectly describe what is important for a healthy and emotionally connected life. Let me share with you:

"Several studies found that people's level of satisfaction with their relationships at age 50 was a better predictor of physical health than their cholesterol levels were."

"...the key to healthy aging is relationships, relationships, relationships."

"Taking care of your body is important, but tending to your relationships is a form of self-care too."

"The people who were most satisfied in their relationships at age 50 were the healthiest at age 80."

"Loneliness kills"

"The study showed that the role of genetics and long-lived ancestors proved less important to longevity than the level of satisfaction with relationships in midlife, now recognized as a good predictor of healthy aging"

All evidence points to **quality** relationships, not the number of people in your life, and quality means the **amount of trust and vulnerability established and nurtured.** These relationships buffer us from life's impacts and aging. Having someone you trust and who trusts you pays off in every way. Relationships protect brains — memories stay sharper longer due to retelling stories and bodies stay healthy and active.

One final point on relationships: it is important to

know that quality relationships don't necessarily need to be smooth all the time. There can be conflict — just that you can count on the other person when times are rough.

The idea of a typical tough business person, living life as a loner and driving a hard bargain at work may be doing more harm than good. In past decades, many young adults were often encouraged to: "figure it out by themselves" or to "go it alone" or even "you don't need anyone else but you." In specific instances, these are acceptable points. But, over a lifetime, where will this lead the child if they focus solely on this teaching? According to an article in The Atlantic newsletter, "Men who scored highest on measurement of warm relationships earned an average of $141,000 a year more at their peak salaries (usually between ages 55 and 60) than the men who scored lowest..."[3] Accordingly, there must be balanced, supportive conversation with the children in your life about how to form and nurture relationships.

Close relationships pay off in all manners in your life, starting at childhood and leading through your peak earning years and into your 80s. We have research-based proof that close rapport with others is the key to living a healthier life. Therefore, this poses some important questions we will examine:

- What constitutes close community in an individual's life?
- What is the reason so many struggle with loneliness and lack of connection?

In conclusion, loneliness issues absolutely exist, we

all feel it in our life. We have decades long research from Harvard and know how to combat loneliness. Therefore, what is the reason we don't undertake the task? We know the answer and it is to foster relationships in our community. What is the reason we don't seek or create it? In my years of working in personal growth and research for this book, I've discovered that individuals decide to become and remain speechless. To convey it another way, a large percentage of our population has chosen **silence** in one form or another and decided that the depth of personal interactions will be minimal.

# SILENCE IS VIOLENCE
PUNISHING SILENCE

I want to increase your awareness of Punishing Silence in your life and show you the costs of using it in your relationships and community. You may believe you only use silence in specific cases with your partner, friends, family, children or community. However, if you utilize it in one area, I'm confident you employ it on many and differing occasions. The impact is devastating to those involved, and as the years pass the toll becomes larger and more profound. It will impact the depth of the relationship, it will impact your health and it will put distance between you and others. Damage is done every single time punishing silence is utilized.

I believe that Paul Schrodt, PhD said it best concerning Punishing Silence, "Partners get locked in this pattern, largely because they each see the other as the cause." Schrodt continues, "It's a real, serious sign of distress in the relationship."[1]

In this type of silence the violence is not exclusive

towards the individual who caused the pain, because it also impacts you (the person choosing to be silent) and your mind. It robs you of your future by keeping you stuck in the past. As long as you live in silence, you're attached directly back to that event or person where the issue started. No healing has taken place or healing is incomplete. In this sense it is self-violence and there is a steep inner price to pay.

In our closest relationships, silence in an argument, fight or even a disagreement is often seen as taking the high road, being more mature in the relationship and situation. While it might be in a one-off situation, it is also controlling and often meant to inflict pain on the other individual. Using Punishing Silence during every fight turns it into using it for every encounter in which there exists differing opinions and point of view. It is an easy habit to start and a relationship killer in the end. It can bleed over into friendships and your community.

Kipling Williams said, "Excluding and ignoring people, such as giving them the cold shoulder or silent treatment, are used to punish or manipulate, and people may not realize the emotional or physical harm that is being done."[2] Therefore, by combining the factors listed in this chapter I conclude, not in jest, that: **Punishing Silence is Violence to the closest relationship in your life.**

Silence is simply a cover or outward key to the fact that there's a deeper issue. To choose to not risk feeling the pain of "that topic" or somehow a perceived "I'm not going to give in and let them win!" the individual chooses to say nothing at all. It might begin in one area (intimacy, commitment, pain) and over time it will creep into additional topics by creating distance in all areas of the relationship. Who all gets punished in this scenario? Everyone — even you. Your partner can do nothing with nothing, additionally once this game becomes ingrained, then there half of the relationship drains away over the coming months, years and decades. If your partner didn't understand your position/pain/point "back then" do you think they will understand your silence now?

Typically Punishing Silence is utilized under two situations. First, they did something (broke trust, let you down again and again, made poor decisions) and you've had enough. Your commitment to them has ended, cut off forever or as long as it takes to stop hurting. Maybe you've decided you're done with the pain and this is the only manner you know to keep them away from you. Second, you've both hurt each other and you've decided either we hurt each other more or you make the determination to cut off all deep communication. Punishing Silence is an effective way to end communication within the relationship and effectively end the bond even if no divorce papers are signed.

I recall with clarity the exact moment the idea of Punishing Silence entered my life:

I was at home with my family and an individual close to us stopped in to say hi (we will call this person *Alex*). I recall I was not involved in the conversation but was in the room and as the details unfolded it grabbed my attention.

*Alex* started with a story about conflict with their partner. It was a disagreement about a minor topic of having to clean up after each other. However, it was a sore point in the new relationship, and it festered. The story unfolded and it was admitted that the exchange between the couple became more and more tense. Then the partner said to Alex, "I'm too busy -- you stay home all day get with it and **do more**."

*Alex* was still upset by the interaction and my spouse asked, "Well how did you respond?" *Alex* said "I didn't respond and I took the high road. I simply stopped talking. I'm still not talking to them."

Now I was fully involved in this story and situation. I asked, "When did this fight take place?"

*Alex* responded, "Three days ago."

I very clearly remember my stomach rolling over and I replied, "You think you took the high road by not talking to your partner for three days about cleaning the house?" *Alex* was absolutely clear that yes it was the healthiest decision to not speak (i.e. Punishing Silence).

I pointed out that not speaking is a very controlling game in a relationship and for them to consider what the other individual can do when they encounter a wall of silence. Nothing. You can do nothing with nothing. When communication within a relationship stops because of a disagreement, the silence often causes more damage than an honest conversation would.

As we can see in my story above with our friend *Alex*, I acknowledge there are some reasons that might feel valid for moving to Punishing Silence. Many reasons which I've uncovered from talking with those in life and leading personal growth workshops are:

- Stopped feeling, stopped caring, stopped wanting more and decided that silence was the easiest way to interact, shut down
- Inward focused and see only their issues not those of the partner, closed off to the world
- Decided not to trust, hurt once bad and decided to never trust again, if you don't talk, no one knows you and they can't hurt you again
- Think I can solve my own problems though my silence
- Think keeping the "silent" home is some type of solution

As stated above all of these are valid sounding; however no growth of the relationship takes place in these mindsets. Think back in time, what were your greatest dreams for the relationship? To sit and have deep conversations and explore topics of great importance? To speak openly about life and challenges face to face? To support each other on the journey of life? When your relationship began it was meant to be one of deep bonding and supportive conversation.

The short term goal of Punishing Silence is to create distance between yourself and your loved one by not saying the words. As the years pass, they can perceive something is keeping you at a distance, but they can only guess as to what it is. What might seem obvious to you might not be as obvious to them. Too often they give up, give in and move on. You're left in silence that has no ending, all along choosing to wait for a precise event or action from your partner which you've decided is needed to end or heal the pain.

This can be expanded to include not only your partner and families but also your larger community. If you're holding yourself back and spending a lot of mental energy on silence and punishing, then you cannot fully engage in your community. It is obvious to all that the relationship is rocky and no one wants to be involved on a deep level.

The long-term game of Punishing Silence seems to be incredibly impactful at instilling fear in the other partner. This may be because the other individual often goes to the worst-case scenario for the relationship and causes — lack of intimacy, doubts of self-worth, breaks trust. Whatever difficult past experience an individual has had in a relationship will be brought to the surface and re-experienced. With the lack of a verbal check-in with the mate, the other individual has to make it up in their mind.

It's not necessarily only about the silence, but it is also about what is not being said. To express it another way; the topic that is the root cause is not discussed in a constructive healing manner. Sadly, punishing silence (in a detrimental form) delays any type of outcome, let alone a healthy state of relationship, and impacts both individuals.

Finally, Punishing Silence is contagious and the first person likely to catch it after you is your partner. Silence seems to spread somewhat easily within a relationship. I cannot imagine a more damaging set-up between two that have sensitive and important issues which need resolution, and both parties are using silence. It is complex, there are now three organisms that have to overcome silence all at the same time: Partner #1, Partner #2, and the Relationship entity. All three have to be in alignment or nothing happens. All along, the children are watching and learning every step of the way how to deal with conflict and wounds.

Paul Schrodt, PhD Professor of Communication Studies, reviewed 74 relationship studies which involved more than 14,000 participants. "the silent treatment is 'tremendously' damaging to a relationship. It **decreases relationship satisfaction for both partners**, diminishes feelings of intimacy, and reduces the capacity to communicate in a way that's healthy and meaningful."[3]

It may have taken one bad decision by one individual

to cause Protective Silence to be used. **It will take both individuals to speak openly and to stop the cycle to heal the relationship.** Punishing silence is not your answer.

## PUSH LOVE AWAY
### PROTECTIVE SILENCE

" Lying is done with words, and also with silence.

— ADRIENNE RICH

What do you believe is the reason you don't fully embrace community, your partner, and instead create roadblocks that keep deep personal connection at bay?

Partner 1: "How are you today?"
Partner 2: "I'm fine." (followed by silence)

The biggest obstruction is your choice to use **silence to hide your pain and fears.** This is not about a form of peaceful silence, this type of silence is about you thinking *I'm never going to utter a word about this part of who I am or my past* or *I'll not even engage in the topic just to keep myself safe from a chance I'll have to speak about it.*

**As the silence grows inside you, so do your fears.**

A person who chooses to never say the words and explore the past situation creates a breeding ground for their fears. These fears, with time, grow and spread and lead to confining decisions for yourself and others. In these fears, you can find ample reasons to not embrace and grow in community, and rely on the use of silence to push others and love away.

Protective Silence is often a manner in which to control. It could be to control oneself from engaging in a conversation, having a discussion with an individual, thereby controlling another individual. I suggest there are many different forms of protecting "silence." The alternative forms it can take are:

- Non-stop verbal talking
- Constant state of busy
- Quickly moving to anger
- Avoiding topics/individuals
- Not engaging in deep relationships
- Engaging in only small talk topics

All of these are very effective ways to create a general state of silence about a certain topic in life. When you use them in your relationships, there is little others can do to engage on a deep level. Alan Burdick of The New Yorker reports, "Yes, there are occasions when you have to actively steer conversations away from the rocks..."[1] All this just to avoid "that topic," imagine the mental and emotional energy and stress required to create distance just to keep your secrets safe.

Whatever you do, don't think about a white bear. The original observation of the White Bear thought experiment came from Fyodor Dostoevsky in 1863 and was published in his "Winter Notes on Summer Impressions." Later Daniel Wegner, PhD, a psychology professor at Harvard and founding member of thought suppression took it a step further.[2] Dr. Wegner designed an experiment where individuals were asked to verbalize their stream of thought and not think about a white bear. Every time the white bear came to mind they rang a bell. Results showed that they rang the bell more than once a minute.

Dr. Wegner titled this "ironic processes," where he describes it as individuals telling their mind not to think about X. A part of the mind avoids those thoughts. Another part of the mind checks-in on the thought to make sure it is not coming up. Thereby bringing it to your mind! For us this means, just because you decide to stay in silence doesn't mean you're hiding or avoiding anything. "It" is all there inside you, and not talking about the topic doesn't make it go away. I think of it as a bit of self-imposed torture to sit in silence and allow your thoughts to focus on the piece of past you most want to put away.

Dr. Wegner proposes a number of suggestions on how to remedy this situation. However, one in particular is important for us. It is titled "Exposure." Dr. Wegner states "This is painful, but it can work." Basically, **Exposure** is the opposite of silence. It is about breaking out the stories, thoughts, and past to expose them so that they lose part of their power over your mind. Then you'll be able to think and focus less on the White Bear. We cause ourselves so much internal violence in the now by allowing silence to be the default and avoid.

Avoiding the interaction, conversation, and thoughts by using silence does not work for you. It is the white bear thought experiment; as long as you tell yourself to not think about "it" and move to silence then your helpful mind will keep checking in on "it" to make sure you're not bringing it up there by mentally bringing it up! Life brings us pain, and when you choose to leave it there in the past, it will continue to bring you pain. It will grow like a weed, continually coming back up — polluting your life and relationships. Choose to expose the pain, talk about things that matter to you, choose to speak up and start to move past your history. Only when you Create Value from the past and speak about it do you create a powerful memory, and it, in turn, helps you grow.

I believe that healthy conflict is a part of growth and as long as you're moving in a healthy direction, speaking respectfully, listening to the other position and working to resolve the issue. The relationship can become stronger and more healthy. Protective silence leads to more silence.

Silence is proof that something deep down needs to be spoken. Silence is the choice to keep it deep down in a dark place. By staying silent, you limit the amount and the extent of interaction and connection. It keeps words, thoughts, ideas, dreams, potential solutions bottled up. There's no opportunity to obtain outside solutions or a different way to approach a difficult situation. Silence is violence and mainly on the health, heart, and psyche of the person engaged in the act.

Individuals I've interviewed have justified their use of Protective Silent as a defense, not considering it a controlling manner to fight in a relationship. I acknowledge there are some reasons that seem valid for moving to Protective silence:

- Broke silence once, shared and it didn't go well, or like they wanted it to go, therefore they decided to play the shallow safe game of silence
- Think they can solve their own problems internally, still working on them with little progress
- Think keeping their "silence" is some type of solution
- "I didn't want to hurt their feelings or mine."
- "I knew they would not listen to my voice."
- "I did it out of love for them and wanted to save them the burden."

As stated above, all of these seemed like valid solutions, but with Protective Silence, it spreads and infects more areas and varied topics within you. It can become a dark hole that is tough to escape.

So this is my "exposure" for Protective Silence:

I'm an individual who has been diagnosed with Dyslexia.

As early as I can remember in my school life, I loved the first three or four years of school. I can pinpoint memories today that stand out which might have given clues to challenges that were coming, but at the moment I was not aware. One moment in the first grade was a trip with my class to the school library. We were encouraged to select a book to take back to class for the day. I recall my best friend choosing (from my child's point of view) a book with mostly words and few pictures, and I wanted all pictures in my books. It was a confusing moment.

That was just an early sign that more challenges were on the horizon. I excelled in school and placed above average when I hit 3rd grade, but then my standardized test scores fell quickly. After numerous attempts, my parents finally found the correct diagnosis for me when I was 7 or 8 years old. From that point forward, I did my very best to hide the fact and never let anyone know what was going on.

I believe I spent a large amount of energy "hiding" in classes so I would not be seen as different from my friends and peers. The issue was that I knew I was different. When I compared my handwriting to others in my class... I was different there too. I could see it in my spelling — I never made a 100 percent and had it posted, in glory, on the classroom wall like my best friend. I could experience it at the speed I read. I was different and everyone else was smarter, better, and more skilled than me. That was the absolute story I told myself.

My challenge with dyslexia continued through high school into college. I dreaded, avoided, and at times refused to speak with my professors about my dyslexia and how it impacted me in class.

I feel strongly that the protective silence had the following impacts on my health and friendships: I had a high stress level starting in grade school, I robbed myself of closer relationships by withholding facts about who I was. Holding back in the classroom allowed me to hide pieces of my weaknesses and faltered growth of strengths.

Now, as an adult, when I reflect on when I did share with a friend or teacher, every time they were understanding and helpful, however I still had a more powerful internal story and was committed to use as much energy as I could to keep it hidden.

Looking back, I see the stress it put on me and my life. I know that it put me in a negative frame of mind when approaching school, and relationships within school. The place I played the biggest price was in my relationship with myself. I didn't like or accept myself 100 percent, because I believed none of my friends and schoolmates did either.

Only when I entered Graduate School (in my late 20s) and started having professional and educational successes did I start to break the silence, as painful as it was at first. I told my closest friends. I spoke openly with my professors and administrators. All of them were supportive. I realized that was the biggest fallacy of my past beliefs and story I made up. I thought people would push me away, make fun of me, know my deepest darkest secret. The truth is that the opposite happened. I not only found support. I found community too.

I'd wasted a lot of energy from 8 years old to my mid-20s. The pinnacle of my Create Value in life and smashing "the secret" and silence happened when I created a speech, applied, and was accepted (with my younger sister who holds two Doctoral degrees) to give a speech at the largest dyslexia conference in the world (we gave it on multiple occasions).

At 30, I'd finally turned my silence around and gave it a voice and felt free. I'd created a larger and closer community for myself.

We connect with others through our vulnerability and openness, not our strengths. As long as I was showing only strength in my classrooms, no one could connect, they felt less than (like I was feeling with others). When I opened up and broke my silence and became vulnerable, people could connect through their own weaknesses and then we could have a deep conversation.

The same is true for making new connections in your community. If you enter an engagement and only show strength, then new relationships are limited. When you are open, and people get to know the true you, then there is a powerful chance for internal and relationship growth. Silence is the killer of relationship, and therefore community, so I ask what brings a group of individuals together to create community? It is some form of commonness. What pushes the individual away from the community? It involves a form of lack of commitment, lack of interaction, and self-isolation. **The community isn't necessarily ended, however the individual's participation might be.**

The use of silence to disengage is an excuse, a dangerous trap. It is the Either/Or mindset trap. Either I open up and have to talk about everything that hurts, or I go silent. In truth, there are an unlimited number of options and healthy steps to be taken to have the conversation and say the words.

**Make no mistake. The act of Silence is not an act of love, but an act of cutting off love.**

Protective Silence does not bring you closer to the other person (nor yourself); it damages them and the relationship. It is an incredibly effective way to 1) control your emotions (which leads to lack of emotion); 2) move the other individual to a worst-case scenario, (many individuals turn to this type of scenario when they lack information); and 3) give the appearance as the "good" one in the relationship — the one who acts nice and sweet and never fights.

Protective Silence is sure to break community/relationships/friendships and increase **loneliness, not only in the individual but everyone involved.** When you go silent, everyone loses out on your knowledge, learning, words and insights. The biggest price of all is the internal turmoil. I hope I have your attention that it is not a right thing to do; it is not taking the high ground. It damages all involved. It may start with a close relationship, then to a group of friends, then a group of co-workers and community. How you do anything is how you do everything. One conversation at a time leads to a lifetime of conversation.

## WHEN SILENCE EQUALS SECRETS

I'd come across the Grant and Glueck study (the Harvard research tracking alumni and Boston men living in poverty) numerous times in my life. I found it interesting, insightful and thought that it would slowly start to turn the ship so that as a society we'd become more focused on our relationships. As time passed, it has not happened and, in my opinion, the opposite has been true and more individuals became isolated and lonely. As I researched the study and read on the topic, I understood loneliness was becoming a vital issue in our culture. I've long pondered, "What is the reason for this?" I've determined it's due to people deciding to live in silence (and bypassing vulnerability). The next logical question for me: What is the reason individuals are choosing to be silent when there are so many positively impactful reasons to be open? I came to an uncomfortable determination; the reason we are silent is that we want to **protect** our secrets and emotional self.

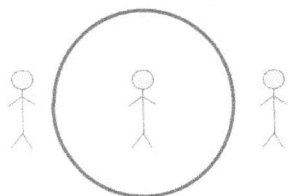

**Loneliness** is created by choosing to **live in silence** and you choose to be silent because you have **painful secrets** which you don't ever want to speak about again and would prefer to never think about in your life.

First, let's establish what is a secret. According to Merriam-Webster dictionary [1], a secret can be defined as one or all of the following (**emphasis mine**):

- kept from knowledge or view
- marked by **the habit** of discretion
- working with hidden aims or methods
- not acknowledged
- designed to **elude observation** or detection

Also synonyms provided by Merriam-Webster that include covert, hush-hush, sneak, stealth, undercover, underground, underhand, underhanded. Finally, a few antonyms, such as open, overt and public.

The reason you move to silence and don't embrace community fully is to keep **your secrets.** You cause yourself so much pain in the now by allowing secrets to rule and avoiding the discomfort of your past. It starts small but slowly infests area by area of life. At first only the biggest secrets are hidden away, then uncomfortable topics, then differing opinions, then dreams, then goals, then needs and wants. It is not that one area of communication is cut off, rather that communications become cut off.

> Nothing haunts us like the things we don't say.
>
> — MITCH ALBOM

I have empathy for you and individuals with painfully traumatic events in their history. It is perfectly reasonable that you use silence in your closest relationships. There are things you don't want to say, past events you don't want to experience, and images you never want to see again in your mind's eye. While it is reasonable on the surface, on a deeper level, when you choose to stay in silence about those types of past events, the result is that they will haunt you daily.

What would you never post on social media? What would you never tell your best friend? What would you never tell your spouse? Secrets vary tremendously; what one person might believe is a big dark secret, another would think minor. What a friend could forgive and look past, to a spouse it could cause deep pain.

Olivia Petter reports, based on a Columbia University survey, that there are 38 common secrets. Findings from the survey report that "... 96 per cent of participants were withholding a secret." The makeup of those secrets are: Hurting (physically or emotionally) another individual, Drug use/habit, Physically harming yourself, Having lied to someone.[2] What are yours? What causes you to move to silence versus bringing secrets to the light of day?

> Nothing makes us so lonely as our secrets.
>
> — PAUL TOURNIER

How much energy are you using to hide them? Hiding, living in the fear of being judged, steering conversations, avoiding — all of them create distance. Consider all the conversations you didn't have, didn't fully engage in, all the topics you diverted because you wanted to avoid any opportunity of having to share your secret/s (or perhaps someone asking a question about your secrets). When you cut short or avoid conversations in the general arena of a secret, it cuts all deep conversations. Within the motivation to avoid one area, the unintended consequence is dampening the opportunity for deep conversation in other areas.

**In all ways, your secrets lead to silence which leads to distance and loneliness.**

Michael Slepian, PhD, wrote in a Scientific American article, "When we think of a secret, it can make us feel isolated and alone."[3] On the other side no secrets = freedom. We have to move through our secrets and out of silence to reach that state.

Often secrets are thought of as a painful past act carried out (by one's self or another individual), however I suggest they can come in many varied areas. For example, they can come from you feeling undeserving of your hopes or dreams. When was the last time you shared a big dream for yourself with a friend or loved one? All too often old secrets create bad habits which set up not sharing our "good" secrets later in life. It is seen as easier to not share our dreams than have them not come true. Silence due to secrets in one area impacts all areas of your life.

Do you want others to be real with you? Do you want them to share their truths? Do you want others to be real? Where does that state begin? That state of open, vulnerable relationships starts with you acting in that manner. All these key points lead back to the fact there is a secret in you. Which means there's a secret in the relationship. A lack of vulnerability is established and things get quieter and quieter.

You cannot have a new future until you stop re-reading and hiding the past chapters of (the pain in) your life. Is it time to move into your future with a clear and empowering past? Is it not time to have the future you want?

There is no magic moment where the pain is gone, you suddenly feel free, your relationships improve, and the community comes calling. It takes emotional and mental exposure (talking openly) to the past pains and cleans them out. It may take working with a professional, depending on the type of pain.

You have a secret, or you have many secrets, and they are hurting you, your closest relationship and your ability to create and grow your community. **We all do it; it happens to all of us.**

The best experiment I know of to see what role your secrets play in your life is to remove all distractions from your life and sit in silence for as long as possible. When you do this, what comes to mind? Where does your mind wander? It is an interesting experiment and will tell you what your mind finds really important.

In my previous books, I wrote about my time in the Peace Corps working with small businesses. As I reflect on my time serving there, I often think about the three months spent in training before I went to live in my community. We were told that there would be a high drop out rate of 30 percent during the in-country training. In my group, that was accurate, because I remember doing the math when they told us the statistic, and I tracked it until graduation. Then we were told that there would be an additional 30 percent attrition within the first three months on site in their communities. I found that to be true again.

I didn't understand at the time that people who I thought were better prepared than I was to make the transition had resigned. As I look back, I believe it was a big experiment of what I explained above. There is a lot of time to think when you first move to your site and few distractions of modern society. For most (a vast majority) volunteers, there were no malls, no cell phones, no immediate internet access, no movie theaters, no Netflix, and so on. Instead there were books, conversation with your neighbor, community and yourself.

Left with a lot of time to think, the life experiences that you want to avoid come back over and over again. When you are not distracted, secrets are increasingly difficult to avoid. Alone, all alone with your thoughts... "...secrets were far more likely to come to the fore when people were alone with their thoughts than in a social situation..."[4]

What do you think about when all is quiet? When you can't sleep? When you remove yourself from the noise of life? Do you wonder if "this" will happen again in the future?

If you're looking for an incredible growth opportunity, find a silent retreat. I have friends who've sought them out and experienced a three-day weekend up to ten days of silence! From my point of view, that is some hardcore self-learning and a wonderful opportunity to become clear on where healing needs to take place next in life. When you elect to undertake the growth opportunity of silence, then, as you have realizations, please journal. It is vital to capture your gain in knowledge. With the writings you know where to focus your growth or healing opportunities. Also, after time passes, it is worthy to look back and see how far you've come.

## LAYERS OF SECRETS

According to Author/Editor Bec Crew you have 13 secrets, five of which you've never told a single person. On an individual level, the concern is not having one or a few secrets. What causes you the most problem is the mental energy you'll expend thinking about your secrets (while trying to not think about them).[1] She continues, "When participants were asked to judge the slope of a hill or the length of a distance, those who were preoccupied with keeping a secret judged the hills as steeper and the distances longer than they really were."

How might this apply to you and your life? Consider common long-term stressors in your relationship and life where secrets might be found. You have a teen with behavioral issues that is causing problems in the house. Constant fights with a spouse that are emotionally draining. Work stresses, too much work, not enough work, and/or a boss you don't respect. Problems in the house with finances or intimacy. All of these topics (and more) are potential places for secrets. Any of these factors can cause years, or even over a decade, of stress.

After years of stress, let's return to what Bec Crew says "...those who were preoccupied with keeping a secret judged the hills as steeper and the distances longer..." therefore in your life, you might judge the commute as more stressful and longer. You might overreact to the decision by the teen. The work days may seem like they last forever! All of that energy spent to keep the secret a secret impacts you in how challenging you see your life, for the worse. To state it another way, by keeping a secret over the long term, you're adding stress and fatiguing your mental capacities. Thereby experiencing every challenge as bigger, longer, steeper, tougher.

According to Michael Slepian; "... in adults, secrecy is associated with lower well-being and relationship quality."[2] You must be clear as to what your secrets are and how deep they are buried. As you see there is a huge price to pay for holding secrets, as the secrets get bigger, deeper, and the longer they're held, the greater the cost.

Take an inventory of your life secrets, however you decide to label them: big, small, worrisome, heavy, deep, old, new, and so on. Not a secret that was told to you by someone else, or a poor decision by a mate. Set those aside and focus on your own personal secrets. What are your top three? Does anyone know any of these secrets — spouse? friends? community? How much time and effort do you spend thinking about, or avoiding, the topic or secret? What is your deepest secret? We are going to use those secrets now and dissect them in detail.

**Johari Window**[3]

|  | Known to Self | Not Known to Self |
|---|---|---|
| **Known to Others** | Open Area | Blind Spot |
| **Not Known to Others** | Hidden Area | Unknown |

Johari Window is a fabulous tool to use in many different environments to gain insight into what is known and not known about yourself and surroundings. The key insights come when you identify what is in the four quadrants (Open Area, Hidden Area, Blind Spot & Unknown). Once you have the information, you can decide if that is the manner in which you want to live your life, or if you want to make adjustments.

For our use in *Life Unspoken,* I'll format the Johari Window for secrets:

| Secrets | Known to Self | Not Known to Self |
|---|---|---|
| **Known to Others** | Open Area<br>Vulnerability to those in our life | Blind Spot<br>Distance is often perceived by others, while they don't know your deepest secrets, they know the relationship is closed off |
| **Not Known to Others** | Hidden Area<br>"Dark" Secrets which we keep to ourselves, this area causes us the most issues because we use a lot of mental energy to keep them hidden | Unknown<br>Forgotten/Suppressed memories or secrets, if you believe you have experiences in this quadrant, it is best to seek professional support |

Now is the perfect time to take an inventory and create your own personal Johari Window to understand which of your secrets are living in the four quadrants. It is vital that you're as honest as possible. The payoff for you is a tremendous step towards: 1) starting the healing process, 2) breaking the silence that has encompassed areas of your life for years, and 3) a step towards finding your community and place in this world.

While conducting this exercise, I suggest you start with the Open Area (Vulnerability to those in our life) quadrant.

Open Area — Consider:

- What past secrets are now living in this quadrant?
- Which of your past secrets would you be willing to speak openly about?
- Have you disconnected emotions from your story?
- What secrets do you hold from your spouse? or friends? or community?
- How might you help others if you were truly vulnerable to all in your life so that everyone could see into your Open Area?
- How do you feel about the past secrets that reside in the Open quadrant?

After you've outlined Open Area, then move to the Unknown (Forgotten/Suppressed memories or secrets).

Unknown — Consider:

If you believe there are secrets/memories in this area, it is best to seek professional support to understand what is there and the reasons they are suppressed.

Now the tough work begins. Fill out your personal Johari Window Secret quadrants, onto the Hidden square ("Dark" Secrets which we keep to ourselves, this area causes us the most issues because we use a lot of mental energy to keep them hidden).

Hidden — Consider:

- What secrets do you know for a fact you've locked into your Hidden quadrant?
- Hidden Secrets from Spouse?
- Hidden Secrets from Friends?
- Hidden Secrets from Community?
- If a certain topic was opened by a friend or partner, would you spend a lot of energy changing the subject?
- What topic have you "never told a soul?"
- What secret have you told to only one other person in your life?
- What secret makes you want to physically and emotionally shut down and move to silence? Is it area specific, such as spouse? friends? community?
- With whom do you hold anger when they come to mind? (There are likely secrets in this area)
- When someone new comes into your life, and

they remind you of someone in the past who hurt you, how do you react?

- How do you feel about the past secrets that reside in the Hidden quadrant?

Now the most difficult quadrant to explore — Blind Spot (Distance is often perceived by others, while they don't know your deepest secrets, they know the relationship is closed off):

Blind Spot — Consider:

First, a suggestion; find a close friend who will be honest and ask them for information on how you come across in life. This is a starting place to open discussion, add to make it your own and give you the information you need.

- Do they experience you as distant?
- How do you hold back?
- How would they rate the relationship from 1 to 10?
- Are you easy to talk with?
- What do people assume about you?

Information may be a bit tough to hear, but it is invaluable if you take it to heart and put the changes into your life. Now to the question for you to examine your Blind quadrant:

- How would you rate your relationships with your loved ones?
- What is the reason they are not rated higher?
- What topics do you shy away from with your friends?
- What topics do you try and change when they come up?
- What is your ultimate goal for yourself, for your relationships and your secrets?

The more secrets, the bigger secrets, the deeper secrets, the less vulnerable you are to the loved ones in your life leads to the more distance created and the more shallow the relationships will become. Take your first big steps today to move more secrets into the Open Area and make the quadrant more available to trusted individuals in your life.

As you have fewer secrets and are more vulnerable in life, your payoff will be immense. Possible positive outcomes will be closer relationships, tighter community, less weight on your mind, great healing. Plus, your overall mindset will improve and become a better judge of the "steepness" of hills before you. It will be easier to judge the true distance to and through your next goal and challenge.

Specifically, for me, when I started to open to others about having dyslexia, I spent a lot less energy wearing the mask that said "I'm smart (in all areas)." It allowed me the freedom to demonstrate strengths in some areas and weakness in others -- the truth about me. It brought me closer to friends as they could support me and proved that I could confide in them and it allowed them to open up about some of their learning challenges. The first step is tremendous, but the payoff for sharing your secrets will impact every area of your life positively!

# YOUR SECRETS, YOUR BODY

I find the topic of how secrets impact the physical body enthralling. A secret seems so minor, small and insignificant. People say "Everyone has them" or "It happened so long ago"... yet you pay a price for carrying secrets, not only mentally and emotionally, but also physically. Your body and health is impacted by your secrets and the topics you refuse to speak about.

Here is a small sampling of what happens to your body when you keep secrets, according to an article in Bustle.com[1]: sleep loss, lack of focus, irritability, digestive issues, higher blood pressure, insomnia. Additionally in a Forbes.com article[2]; holding a secret may impact your body: difficulty with memory, loss of appetite, disruption of metabolism, weakened immune system, increased blood pressure, loss of collagen in the skin, etc. Finally in the article "How Secrets Make Us Sick," author Liz Belilovskaya cites research from the University of Texas psychologist James Pennebraker which found that: "People hiding traumatic secrets showed more incidents of hypertension, influenza and even cancer."[3] Where there's a secret and you decide to lock it away, there will be a physical price to pay.

More research, articles, and books cite differing accounts of how, and at what level, secrets impact our physical health. The key point is that they absolutely do hurt your body. The longer and bigger (based on the perception of the secret holder) the secret, the more it will impact you. Only you can take care of yourself and lift the weight of the past.

There is research on the flipside concerning releasing secrets that is impactful. To summarize, you can increase your physical health by unleashing your secrets; you can improve your physical health by releasing past pains. With this knowledge you may, for the first time, acknowledge that you can link a symptom listed in the previous pages to a secret you hold. The good news is appropriately releasing the secret (by speaking to a therapist, professional or trusted individual, for example) is an important first decision to a better physical life. Taken a step further, if you were not carrying around the baggage of withholding secrets and allowed yourself to take steps to become physically healthy, in addition to many mental health benefits, imagine the life you will lead!

To present holding onto secrets in a slightly different manner, keeping secrets is similar to verbally and emotionally shutting down in life and relationships. Your body has a fascinating gland -- the adrenal gland whose job is to give a shot of adrenaline when facing a fearful or dangerous situation. I believe this is an important topic for all and the subject of my first book. (*Fight or Flight: Make Better Decisions to Enjoy Your Life* ).

In relationships, when the Fight or Flight response is utilized, it leads to two distinct states of (one external and the other internal) conflict. The Fight response sets up the same verbal altercation you've had with your partner since the early days in your relationships (you both know it so well that you could step into their shoes and they into yours and you could fight their position). Or it results in Flight, emotionally and verbally shutting down, secrets and all, "It's not worth it." Both of these states have an unhealthy impact on your body, mostly through your cardiovascular system and the stress it places on your vital organs.

Understand there is a physical price to pay for keeping your secrets locked away in your life behind a wall of silence.

# SPOKEN AND UNSPOKEN AGREEMENTS

A key piece of healthy communities and relationships is keeping agreements. When these agreements are not kept or respected, by you or the other half of the relationship, damage is done and often secrets can form out of the pain.

Let's focus on your closest relationship, your mate/partner, in this section. When you entered your committed relationship, there were numerous promises and agreements formulated. In order to keep a relationship healthy and growing, these agreements must be kept, and when broken they must be repaired. Within your relationship, there are two types of agreements: Spoken and Unspoken. Both are equally important.

Some of the most common spoken are:

| Love the person | Protect them | Honor the relationship | Be Faithful |
|---|---|---|---|
| Support | Cherish Them | Listen | Be Respectful |

Unspoken Agreements are also a vital part of a bond. Examples of unspoken agreements are:

| Keep Agreements | Speak Kindly | Be Honest | Act with Integrity |
|---|---|---|---|
| Provide | Speak Openly | Don't Keep Secrets | Be Kind |

All of these agreements strengthen the foundation of the relationship. **Upon entering a committed relationship, Silence is not a Spoken or Unspoken Agreement.** In fact it is the opposite to the cherished agreements listed above.

Spoken agreements contrary to silence are:

| Love | Honor Them | Support | Act with Integrity | Open Communication |
|---|---|---|---|---|
| Be Kind | Be Respectful | Be a Team | For Better or Worse | Share |

Unspoken agreements around silence are:

| Speak the Truth | Open Up | Share Dreams | Support Dreams | Live Life with Passion |
|---|---|---|---|---|
| Be Open to New Ideas | No winning in Arguments | Be honest | Don't keep score | Be Kind |

The good news is that keeping your agreements is a clear cut decision. Either you are or are not working to keep them. Do your part to keep your agreements, keep your relationship healthy, and remain out of silence as much as possible.

## OTHERS' REACTION

" A good friend of mine loves to say: Your head and thoughts are a dangerous neighborhood, don't hang out there alone.

Loneliness, Silence and Secrets may be the most powerful forces hindering your relationship from becoming closer and from ingraining yourself into community. It is time to remove them from your life. All are in your control to have more or less of today.

What reaction is to be expected by others in your life when you move to silence? It turns into a guessing game of what is going on in your mind. I've personally seen and heard many times stories along the lines of, "I thought all was fine in the relationship until it wasn't, and then it was over." When silence is used the other half of the relationship is left to make up the story as to how healthy or unhealthy the relationship is at any point in time.

It is likely that your partner will decide you're about as happy as they are and they are about as happy as they want to be in the relationship. This leaves the relationship firmly stuck in a marginal (at best) setting of health. Worse, as time passes, there is no improvement, no expression of what is needed in the relationship and one (or both) becomes more and more lonely.

Unfortunately, the act of keeping a secret doesn't appear taxing when viewed externally. For your partner, what options are there to address the silence? No one can be beat at "their game." If you're a master of playing the silence game, then no partner can match you. If your secret is deep and dark enough (from your point of view), then no one can pry it out of you. Your partner/spouse can do nothing with nothing. Healthy relationships take two whole, healthy individuals willing to put forth the effort to grow together. Vulnerability will be met with love and acceptance.

Furthermore, they can't be bad enough, start a big enough fight, leave you alone enough, or be enough of the perfect spouse to influence you to drop/quit the silence game. They know something is causing distance in the relationship. They don't have the knowledge to get to the bottom of the cause.

Sooner or later they will move on. This can take many forms; perhaps the relationship will never formally end, but the damage is done to such an extent that the other stops investing in growth. They may leave emotionally, might start to enjoy the silence, and move into their own game.

Life does not stand still. Your relationship will either expand or shrink in all areas. Expansion (i.e., Personal Growth) is not a given, nor an easy undertaking. However, the payoff is abundant and more of what you want in your home. What is your goal for your life and relationships? If not expansion, then the other option is shrinking. We have proof that the more secrets we keep, the more distance there is in our relationships, the more lonely we feel, and become, and our health and life satisfaction suffers (in the short and long term). What are your intentions and the next best step to remove secrets from your union?

Once you've decided to open up and become vulnerable to those around you, a shift will happen. Growth will start and conversations and actions will change. New ideas on how to heal, or deal with the secret, will be presented and created.

Just the act of saying the words will take the pressure off, allow your brain to focus on other important aspects of your life and renew attention on your relationship. Take the step that works for you, open up to your mate, speak to a trusted friend or co-worker, or speak to a counselor. Some find it easier to open to someone not as well known. Attend a seminar, a retreat, a road trip. Find your next best step and speak of your past. It may not all be easy and the reaction of others is impossible to predict. Over time, as you continue your growth, others will follow as they see your payoff. Your relationship will improve once loneliness, silence and secrets are cleared away.

## THE BIGGEST BARRIER

The biggest barrier to you being vulnerable are your fears. Fears of being judged, fear of coming across as weak, fearing deep connection and being let down again, and the fear of feeling less than in the relationship and/or life. Name the fears that keep you from opening up in life and to your loved one. When you name your fear, you'll have a better opportunity to deal with it.

I've been told, "When you need to call someone, that phone weighs about 400 pounds." Why is it so difficult to pick up the phone and call a close friend? Do you doubt they will pick up? No. Do you doubt they care? No. Do you doubt they will listen? No. It is not about them, it is about the fact you do not want to be vulnerable and move through your fears. This is the single biggest barrier to unlocking the box and getting past loneliness, silence and secrets.

Brené Brown, PhD, Professor at the University of Houston, Speaker and Writer (*Daring Greatly* & *Power of*

*Vulnerability*, among others), writes and speaks a lot about shame and vulnerability. The manner in which shame might be related to fear is by the anxiety of someone knowing about a past event, fear of the act happening again, or fear of judgement. The fear often associated with vulnerability is fear of rejection or of feeling unlovable. Brené has two fabulous quotes that I believe set up this chapter:

> Staying vulnerable is a risk we have to take if we want to experience connection.

> What makes you vulnerable makes you beautiful.

The words that impacted and guided me most are: **In my vulnerability lies my strength.** As long as I choose to see vulnerability as a word to avoid in mind and practice, I'm going to keep my secrets locked up where no one can see them.

Brown's first quote about staying vulnerable and making connections, I've personally found it to be 100 percent accurate. Others can perceive when you are not open with them. Likely they will return the favor and also be guarded with their words, stories and/or emotions. This keeps the relationship from finding its true depth. When one is vulnerable, it allows the other to be vulnerable, hence the relationship benefits and deepens through shared stories, experiences, and the ability to see and know the person.

**Silence, and our lack of will to say the words, keep**

us from what we most want for us in life — close inti-mate relationships.

The choice is clear; chose to face your fears and open up or live in ever-distancing relationships. There is a healthy, open relationship waiting for you to fully step into it. Silence is not your friend.

## REASONS TO BREAK SILENCE

There are always choices in life. I acknowledge, at times, that it may not feel as such; it may feel as though silence is the only option. Silence may have been with you a long time — it is not your friend. You have a powerful tool at our disposal in life — the choice of free will. It can be used to drive you forward or keep you where you are. As far as secrets are concerned, and choosing to stay in silence, you know exactly what it will get you in your life and relationships. All the negative impacts that we discussed here, both physical and relationship, can be righted. However, it starts with you and making a different decision to choose to be open.

For Punishing Silence, nothing is solved and nothing is healed. The past will not change through silence. Healing and change will come through words and dealing with the issues. If the silence has been in the relationship for years, or if the wounds are deep, then consider third party support for the relationship. A couples' therapist or group session can start on a healthy first step.

As you open, and healing begins, others will notice the change, observe the benefit and follow your lead. Be a leader in your life and relationships and your payoff will be more than you can imagine. You know what life is like now in silence, and you know that potential gains await you. All that has to happen is to face your fears and say the words.

According to Scientific American, "People report that when sharing a secret with another person, they often receive emotional support, useful guidance, and helpful advice. These forms of support make people feel more confident and capable..."[1] Think for a moment, what feelings do you want more of in your life. Those of closed off or open, alone or close relationships, without input or supported, without direction or leading? Choose to move towards places of strength and vulnerability instead of moving away from your secrets. All of these decisions and outcomes are multiplied by your family relationships, friendships and communities.

For Protective Silence, consider what Michael Slepian says, "The best thing you can do is to talk to someone about it (secret/s)." When you choose to break the silence and get out of your self-constructed comfort zone, then you'll positively impact your future. You have the opportunity right now to lift the dark curtain and bring healing light on yourself and those around you. Make a decision now to find a safe person, therapist or professional, and share one secret. This is the first step to make your life work better for you.

Often lost in the shuffle is the most important relationship of all, the relationship you have with yourself. How you feel about yourself and life will come across to all with whom you interact. How do you want to be seen and carry yourself in this world? Once you have the goal identified in detail, work from the inside out to align your interior actions, thoughts and feelings with your exterior self.

You'll see rewards in numerous areas of your life: Physical, Emotional, Relationship, among others. Today is the day when life begins to improve, with this book and this page.

You may not be aware of the community that awaits you, others who have a similar or same story and pain. Maybe even a completely different story, but your actions will give them permission to be brave too. According to Scientific American, "When people find a healthier way of thinking about their secret, they ruminate less on it, and have improved well-being"[2]

That unknown community can provide new tools, new manners of thinking, and a new support base to go about your life and dealing with your past. That is what community is all about, finding the support of others and using the groups' knowledge to become more.

Back to the beginning of the chapter, it's a choice to stay exactly where you are and keep your secrets buried, which drives you to silence. There is a price to pay for this decision. It is not pleasant or enjoyable. According to Michael Slepian; "The more people think about their secrets, the more ashamed, isolated, and inauthentic they feel."[3] The secrets, the silence, the feelings are barriers to having the best relationships possible.

I'll close this chapter with some powerful words from Frank Warren and his TED talk ,"Half a Million Secrets":

> "I believe secrets are the currency of intimacy, and I think by sharing them we can not only develop stronger relationships with friends and family but maybe get a better understanding of who we are. So I feel secrets are transformative," he continues; "I think the sweet spot, in terms of intimacy, is to share more of the secrets than we feel comfortable with."[4]

In conclusion, your feelings of loneliness are created by your choice to be silent. In life and relationships, the core reason for choosing silence is the motivation to hold and hide your secrets. Breaking the silence will bring you closer relationships, bigger community, better health, and a longer life — those are your 'wow' factors to breaking silence.

## PUNISHING SILENCE
### WHAT TO DO ABOUT IT

I have a picture in my mind of a sweet elderly couple who have been married for 40+ years. One of them makes the decisions: financial, vacations, business, weekend plans, and so on. The other is sick and tired of it, and has been for 38 years, and sits in their chair in silence. Waiting... Waiting... Waiting... to be asked what is wrong. What is one to do about it today so that 38 years don't pass -- in silence?

You must be accountable for how you feel and to express your feelings in a manner in which they can be understood and dealt with constructively. When the ultimate goal of a relationship is intimacy, then the ultimate means in which to create intimacy is to open up and work on the same understanding about the state of the relationship and build greater closeness.

What does giving someone the Punishing Silent treatment communicate in the relationship? I'm not confident in my position. I don't trust you. I don't care enough to make the effort. None of these are true statements, and there may be a lack of safety and trust within the relationship, and forgiveness is needed. The other limiting beliefs will only keep you stuck. Understand your relationship goal and work towards it by creating more **trust and safety.**

When you decide to open up, not all past secrets are meant to be shared with those you see "everyday." There are secrets that are best to be expressed in a more private and/or professional space, allowing for new perspectives and potential solutions to be considered. Start in the safest place possible. Then work through to find a piece of forgiveness and, at the least, understanding.

It is worth taking the steps to create the relationship you want. Punishing silence has never made a couple closer. Nor does it solve the core issue that's not under discussion. Only through dialogue does understanding and healing start and continue.

# PROTECTIVE SILENCE

WHAT TO DO ABOUT IT

What can you do about the monster of silence in your life? There are two sides to the equation — the person in silence and the partner on the other side ready to engage verbally. Here is the heart of the issue. There is something else living in your house, something taking up space in your relationship. Scientific American states that when a secret is shared "...it reduces how often their mind wanders toward the secret in irrelevant moments."[1] Choose to move it out of your life and mind so that you can have more clarity and focus on what is important to you. Is your relationship and the joy of now important to you?

Acknowledging that you use this type of silence in order to avoid is a key step. Now you can prepare yourself **to do something different.** One of the most powerful lessons in growth is knowing that you have the power to take differing action to get what you want. You can choose to heal, stand in confidence, find a trusted place to speak of secrets. Do you prefer to live your life in small talk or speak of topics that matter to you and build your community?

In order for there to be an environment where you feel you can share your secrets and move out of silence, a key attribute must be in place to foster growth. The relationship must feel **safe and trusting** to both parties. Very little will happen in a relationship where these two aspects are not firmly in place and tested. It is up to both individuals to ensure they do their part to create and grow this type of support.

You have to talk. You must converse about your ideas. You must say the words that matter to you. Share your thoughts on topics that matter. Take a step back and evaluate your relationship. Is it safe and trusting? If yes, then make small steps to open up about your secrets. If it is not a safe and trusting environment, then what can you do to make it so? If you believe there are secrets that will hurt your spouse or damage the relationship, then seek outside counsel; seek a professional therapist to assist in discussing the secrets and issues.

Many individuals don't know whether the relationship is safe and trusting. They've never considered the question. Also, they've never tested the waters and only assumed that their partner can't be fully trusted. Now is the time to decide if you're in the relationship you want in your life and how to take the steps to better it.

In the first step, find a topic that's a safe place to start where your mate can support you to open up, share more and find healing. Share something small to check it out, then once that's a success, let it grow to the next topic.

This is a great step to continue to foster a safe and trusting relationship. Also, it gives permission to your mate to discuss their past wounds.

Maybe your mate isn't the right place to start, or maybe there is an area of your life that you can't yet share with them. Find one true friend, share with them, and I bet they share with you. And if you don't have one true friend...

The point above reminds me of an experience which impacted my life and pushed me to speak at depth with those I trust. I was in a workshop and a man was talking about his life. It was somewhat tense; he wanted a more fulfilling relationship. The individual running the workshop asked if they could share some information with the gentleman and he agreed. The facilitator said, and it is still clear in my head..."I experience you as wanting one true friend." The man broke down and buckled over in tears. What this story tells me is that good people want relationships and often don't know how to go about it. Many don't have one trusted friend, or they've never trusted anyone else and don't know if they have those individuals in their life. If you don't have one true friend, then make changes outlined in this book to open up and create deep relationships. As this story demonstrates, we all long for (at least) one true friend.

The benefits of finding, creating and fostering true friendship and safety will be impactful on your life and mind. Slepian explains, "Secrets are largely solitary creatures and can be tamed with company. Talking about it with another person will really go a long way."[2] Yes! This is your goal to bring light to the dark places of your life and secrets. When you pull them out, their power fades!

Safety and trust — you all deserve these protected places in your life. You deserve more than one. You're the one who is tasked with creating and fostering them. Do so now and peace is not far behind.

Note to readers: It is important to know that quality relationships don't necessarily need to be smooth all the time. There can and will be conflict/disagreement/differing opinions. It is vital that you can count on the other person when times are rough.

## HOW TO CREATE SAFETY AND TRUST

The ultimate goal — the end state for you — is to build and maintain relationships that embody safety and trust. In order to get there, you must know where you are in your current relationship. The type of relationship is not important. It can be a spouse, friend, or community. Start by rating the current status of safety and trust in your relationship on a scale of 1–10. Now let's get started on raising that number. Here are some thoughts on how you will improve the quality and depth of your relationships.

As stated earlier, silence can become a habit, a default position to take into a relationship, or used at specific points when difficult topics arise. Now, habits can be changed and replaced with new ways to act. This is where we are heading; learn to speak about things that matter, join in the conversation of difficult topics and then acknowledge when a weight has been lifted, the relationship improved, safety and trust have been deepened.

The first best step may be to focus on one relationship

at a time to expand safety and trust. Consider starting with your closest relationship and build it to the next level. With this person (and these steps can be applied with all relationships), find the starting point on the staircase (image below). Then endeavor to move up the steps, conversation after conversation, over time. It is important that you emotionally capture the benefits you received by opening up and talking.

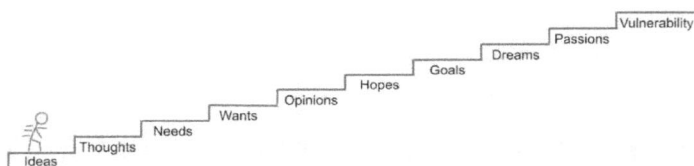

How to begin speaking about ideas, thoughts and opinions? My favorite tool in this respect is to ask questions. Make small talk for a few minutes, then ask that person for their insight on an idea of yours. Ask them for their thoughts about a challenge you're experiencing in your life. If you're really ready to go for it, find a safe person, and ask them to listen as you talk about a challenge you are facing in your life.

If, at this time, it is all too much to take on, one powerful option that doesn't involve others in your life is journaling. Sharing secrets in an anonymous form can be a dress rehearsal for your next best step of sharing it with a friend, partner, or a therapist. It may give you the confidence to take the next step towards a healthier lifestyle.

Relationships get rocky at times; they all are tough. In those times, it is of great advantage to reflect on the reasons you love and fell in love with that person. Those reasons are more important than the difficulties. In a moment of calm, make a list of ten reasons you fell in love with them. Additionally, make a list of ten more things you love about them today. It is for you, no need to share it, but know you have it when you hit the rough patches, and use it. This activity guarantees to help you to acknowledge that safety and trust are alive and well in those challenges.

Another activity to build trust and safety is to focus on the reasons you're grateful for your partner and the relationship. Make a list of three things you're grateful for every evening. Also, when the work day is done, discuss what was the best part of the day, what you're grateful for during the day.

Some of these activities seem minor, but over time the little actions will impact the focus and direction of the relationship. Open up and speak about the blessings in your life; your relationship is a blessing, treat it as such. Finally, **don't confuse the act of talking about anything with talking about things that deeply matter to you and others** – it is a crucial distinction.

## AS YOU OPEN, THEY WILL OPEN

As you open up in your key relationships, so will those trusted individuals. Openness and vulnerability creates its own momentum. Be prepared and have the mindset to allow the other person to say what they need to say to break the silence.

There are a couple of universal open-ended questions that will engage your relationship and lead to deeper conversation. They are: "What do you think about..." and/or where appropriate: "What do you feel about...". They can both be used as stand- alone questions or in tandem. Typically I ask the "think" question before the "feel."

While I think the first two suggested questions are helpful, here's my favorite question of all:

Tell me more about...

OR

Tell me more about that...

It is wide open and allows the person speaking to say whatever they need to say. I use it as a check, when I observe the other individual in deep thought or emotion and they pause. I check in with myself: Are there unanswered questions? Have I drained the story of important points? Additionally, it is honoring the other person to allow them to say whatever they want or need to say.

This next point is going to take some thought on your behalf. While someone is speaking to you, what is the opposite of listening? Talking? No, incorrect answer. The opposite of listening is thinking about what you're going to say in response. Often we want to have our next question ready, debate a point, think we know where they are going in the story. The best practice with someone you want to create closer ties with is to listen. Don't worry about your next question, don't challenge what they are saying till they finish. Listen.

Then I W.A.I.T., if there is just something I feel I must say, I use the acronym W.A.I.T.

**W**hy
**A**m
**I**
Talking

If my goal is only to have my voice heard, to satisfy my ego, it's that I believe my thoughts are really important. I internally decide W.A.I.T. and then make the decision how best to move forward, to speak or not.

It's vital to ensure you're giving the loved ones in your relationships the space to speak. Some people have a lot of words, some fewer, however quantity doesn't equal quality. If you fill up the conversation with your words, it can have the unintended consequence of limiting their participation in the conversation and creating a silent partner.

These are only a few ideas on how to honor another individual and to keep the conversation going. Keep talking about important topics, create silence and room for others to speak, speak up and all will feel heard and valued.

## EMBRACE COMMUNITY

Now is the moment to find your community. It will take time; it will take some trial and error, and it will take you to acting in an open and vulnerable manner until you truly are vulnerable. It will build relationship by relationship 'til you're suddenly surrounded by your peers. It will not just happen; you must be committed. Those in your life today are waiting and rooting for you to open up. They want a deeper connection with you and they know only you can accomplish it.

**Connection takes commitment.**

Returning to the feeling of loneliness in all individuals, consider the thoughts of Dr. Elizabeth Dunn, professor at University of British Columbia. She writes, "talking to strangers makes people feel more cheerful, behave more pleasantly, and believe they belong in a community."[1]

I've experienced this on numerous occasions in personal growth workshops. I attended a men's weekend workshop and was assigned a tiny hotel room with 2 beds and three other men I didn't know. We slept, ate, and attended the workshop for three days together and spoke and shared about topics I've never thought nor shared with anyone else. What I've learned for myself, and from others who've attended similar seminars and workshops, is that after it's complete, people understand that we all have painful and difficult stories to share. There is a bonding opportunity when we share them with others and people still liked, loved, and respected me after I told them one of my "secrets."

According to Kendra Cherry, "Since 1985, the number of people in the U.S. with no close friends has tripled."[2] She continues, "Having just three or four friends is enough to ward off loneliness and reduce negative health consequences..." There it is, you have your goal. Three or four friends to keep loneliness at bay and reap positive health benefits.

When I speak at men's groups, I strongly encourage the men to have two or three other men with whom they can speak about anything. I estimate 20 percent of men in those groups have other men to turn to in their life. The others want it, they know there is something missing, and they don't know how to go about it.

Start by talking about the weather and coffee, and move yourself and the conversation deeper. This will help you and others to create a sense of not feeling alone. Maybe the relationship is one conversation, a few meetings in a year. All have value and are a blessing in your life. Stay committed to building your community and remaining open with your words.

There are numerous theories as to the root of lack of community involvement today. More physical distance from others, smaller families, more technology, society norms, and the list can go on and on. It will be different for each person who answers the question. What is your answer to the question why there is less community involvement in your life?

While the answers are different, the solution is the same on how best to remedy the circumstance. Embrace the community that encircles you. Embrace the community that is waiting with open arms. Embrace community and you'll be embraced. The idea is simple: the reward is immediate, and the pay-off grows over time. The challenge is **you opening up and speaking your truth, ideas, goals, dreams and passions.** All the while knowing that you'll face disagreement and differing opinions.

**Disagreement doesn't equal rejection; agree to disagree and move on.**

It is one thing to mentally understand the quote above, and another to feel it and live it when interacting with a loved during an intense verbal interaction or fight. As I'm sure you agree about your closest relationship, of course my loved one deserves to have their own opinions (my head and heart say). Of course I want to hear it when we are in disagreement (my head says). Of course it is uncomfortable when the words leave their mouth (my heart says). Honestly, it stings and I become a bit fearful in the moment to feel the intensity and directness of the counter-point. All told, the fact that I create a space for my loved ones to be heard, and I respect their independent thoughts is more important than the fact that we disagree.

What you're looking for in the community is belonging. It is the key attribute to any relationship. You want to feel that you belong in the relationship, and group, and hence you want others to belong too.

The Harvard Grant Glueck study (that tracked Harvard alumni and Boston men living in poverty) has fantastic points for us to consider on how to embrace community and ourselves. If you need a to-do list to focus on, this could be a fantastic place to start. How do we accept and create more love in life?[3]

1. Love yourself
2. Conduct loving acts for others
3. Focus Energy on where you and others excel

We will take an in-depth look at each one below.

1. Love yourself, identify your deepest secret and work at forgiveness until a sense of neutrality arrives, make a list of your strengths, engage in an activity that you enjoy. What factors would you take into consideration to determine if someone loves themself? Once you have the list, apply it to yourself and life. One key aspect would be

physical health and the corresponding decisions/actions necessary to stay healthy. Also, if they go beyond the minimum needed, and improve their bodies daily or weekly. A key point might be how they manage their finances. Is it a point of strength or stress in their lives? Then there is balance, principally work-life balance. Is there balance or an attempt at balance in their life? Now your turn. How would you rate how much you love yourself in the same categories: mental health, physical health, finances, and life balance?

Love is a commitment; to love yourself is a commitment to improve the relationship for the rest of your life. Each one of the four categories from above are pillars of life. When one is pushed to the side (or forgotten), it will weaken and cause issues in the other pillars. Start by giving your love for yourself a grade, then grade each pillar. Do you love yourself? If yes, then work on strengthening your foundation.

2. Conduct loving acts for others. Cherish your relationships and add value to them; you must give and receive. There are times in every relationship where we give and receive. It completes a circle. If you only give and never receive, then you've left the other individual with no opportunity to do the same, robbing them of the joy of giving too. The beautiful small acts will keep the relationship healthy and growing.

There are numerous manners in which to give: through a kind act (make coffee, run an errand, support a leader), give your time (take the children for an afternoon, volunteer, sit and listen over a coffee), say "the words" (kind statement, look at someone in the eye and say" thank you," speak up when there's a wrong). All will show the other person that you cherish them in your life. Here is a bonus for yourself and them, after you've completed the loving act, then communicate it to them verbally. "I did 'X' because I love you" or "I did 'X' because I respect you/cherish our friendship." Say the words; only positive can come out of it.

3. Focus Energy on where you excel, not where you lack (What healthy activity do you enjoy? Do you love to bake/exercise/spend time with friends/journal? How much time do you spend in the activity? Whatever it is you love, make time.). The world and life rewards your strengths, and it is important to nurture those areas as you live and push yourself to the next level of success. Do more of what you're good at and where you find joy. This will create more energy to feel and use successes in other areas.

Embrace your community, all of your communities, and the reward will be tenfold in what it provides you in return. Take care of yourself so that you can take care of others; studies prove that this will give you the fullest most healthy life.

Finally, I have a personal plea for you to openly share with your "community" (mate, friends, children, co-workers, volunteer organizations, churches, etc). I believe you are full of knowledge and wisdom that is meant to be shared with others in your life. I believe it so strongly that I dedicated an entire book (*Wisdom is the Beginning: A Better Life Starts with Knowledge*) to the topic. Life is too short to learn every lesson ourselves. By sharing the knowledge gained from others, people have the ability to learn, see life's challenges and create a new outcome for themselves when events are really tough. You have more wisdom than you're aware of; spread it wide and more will benefit.

## MOTION INFLUENCES EMOTION

I admit at times that I don't feel emotionally invested in getting off the couch. I could easily open that application on my phone and watch a few more episodes. I'm also very aware where that will lead me in the day... to more of the same. As I spend my days, I spend my life. I've asked myself many times: How do I start? Where do I start?

It always starts with me. It always starts with you. It starts with you and your commitment, attitude, energy, and mood. It is of the utmost importance that there is congruence within yourself and your exterior feelings. When someone is in congruence, then they are more believable with their feelings and words. Therefore, how do you start to do something that you don't really want to do? Or begin a conversation that feels uncomfortable? Or say words that you'd prefer remain unsaid? With this as a starting place, how do you move toward being in congruence? For if your mind is full of uncomfortable feelings of stories you'd prefer to leave alone, what are the chances of coming across as congruent?

Motion influences emotions, your physical movement can greatly influence your emotional state.

As I sit on the couch, my physical and mental self are congruent. There is a lack of energy, there is little emotion, there is no drive. As soon as I decide to physically move my body, I start to change my mental and emotional state. Which, in turn, will propel my physical state.

The really amazing part is when I feel emotionally down, a fabulous step is to move my body.

- Use this to your advantage and set your emotions on a positive path.
- Use this to influence you to set up time with a friend.
- Use this to your benefit to get a hug.

There is an incredible amount of research about what physical touch does to an individual and how beneficial it is to our health.[1] We, as humans, need physical touch, we need it for emotional closeness. Some need it more frequently than others. Have you ever asked your loved one how many hugs they need in a day to feel complete? For a group of people, they can question the stability of the relationship if their touch "quota" is not being reached. Ask your loved one how many they need, then give it to them! The pay-off can be immense, even if you're not a hugger.

Once you know the number of hugs a day your loved

one needs, now it is time to learn how long to hug. There is a lot of science concerning how long to hug. There are numerous studies that say 20 seconds[2], at that point endorphins are released by the brain. This lowers stress and can assist with numerous health benefits for both.

A man who attended a seminar I held admitted he'd not treated his relationship, marriage and wife well for years and was 100 percent accountable that he'd messed up. He took it upon himself to do all he could to get the marriage on the path to healing. He was not a hugger, didn't grow up in a family that engaged in much physical touch, and never considered that there was value in it. He was challenged to go home, and every day to 1) tell his wife what he loved most about her that day 2) give her a 20- second hug.

He agreed, but the first day back from the seminar he did nothing and the relationship experienced no improvement. He heard a voice in the back of his head that said "you agreed to tell your wife every day what you loved about her, and give her a 20-second hug."

The next morning, after the normal long period of silence, he was preparing to leave for work and he decided "it starts today." He approached his wife, told her what he loved most about her and gave her a hug. He said it was uncomfortable at first, like hugging a stiff board. Over the next few months, he said she'd learned to be more comfortable with the activity and the hugs improved. However, the relationship didn't suddenly become magnificent. He'd taken years to weaken the marriage, and so he knew it would take more than weeks or months to heal.

One morning he climbed into his pick-up to head to work. In his mind he was prepping for a big meeting and project deliverable that morning. He looked up before he started the vehicle and there was his wife at the driver's side window. She said, "Did you forget something today?" He'd forgotten to say what he'd loved most about her and given the hug. The relationship only improved from that point and the key point was when he'd keep his agreement.

There are numerous types of appropriate physical touch that can improve a relationship. A handshake can be a perfect manner (I suggest a warm handshake will be more bonding, where you place your left hand on top of the hand you're shaking), and depending on circumstances, a slap on the back or shoulder bump can work well. Find what works for you and the other individual and then do more of it.

One final story about hugging. My grandmother attended a workshop long ago on physical touch and hugging. She was **not** a hugger but could understand the value. When she left the program, she decided she was going to hug someone new every day. She owned a small business and wanted to create a more welcoming work environment for the staff and clientele.

She picked the person she thought would most appreciate a hug. She asked them and they agreed, and she thought *this isn't so bad*. The next day she found someone new, and the next as well. Then a realization came to her that the people she'd hugged the days before wanted their daily hug. So the number of hugs built. Quickly she had to find someone new. There was a solitary repairman who she tracked down and asked if she could give him a hug. He agreed. Then quit the next day!

The act of hugging brought the staff closer, and no doubt had health benefits for all. It worked for my grandmother. Hugging might not be the answer for your situation, but you can find an appropriate way to show people you care.

## MUST BE HONEST

Honesty is where it all begins. You must be honest with yourself in all areas and situations, then be honest with others. Honest about your past, with the secrets you hold, with the current state of your relationships, with the next best steps. In those truthful answers, you'll find the starting place for your healing. Often avoidance is used to not deal with (or think about) secrets. At this point, we know very well that doesn't work. Secrets win, they come up again and again which drives us to silence.

When you're not honest with yourself, then the true you gets further and further from the surface and is more difficult to find. As years pass, the genuine you doesn't magically appear, it only becomes more ingrained. Little by little, the joys of life dull, relationships fade, and the authentic you is lost.

A new powerful you is waiting to arise and be exposed. Where do you start? Where do you turn the ugliest part of your past to the positively impactful story of the future? Find your honest answers to the questions in this book about your secrets and past, take on the Johari Window exercise, and the long lost you will rise again.

When you make the commitment to be 100 percent honest with yourself and ask and answer really fabulous questions, change will start inside of you.

The ultimate goal to open up about your secrets is two-fold. First, it is to create value out of your past challenges. We will discuss that as our final step in the next two chapters. Second, then your job is all but done when you tell the stories of your secret/s, and within the story there is no emotional attachment. It is just another story about you long ago.

You may need to tell it many times in many situations, but when this environment is reached, then you know you've obtained vulnerability and your relationships with people and community will improve. There is a bright future waiting for you. Your openness and leadership will create the space for others to do the same.

Your dream relationships are there to be created and enjoyed for the rest of your life. Imagine the power and joy that is available to you through these beautiful connections by your side.

## CREATE VALUE
### AND MOVE FORWARD

Create Value is one of the most powerful and empowering principles of personal growth. It is so powerful that individuals who are struggling with the thought of how to start the forgiveness process might want to consider working to Create Value first. I've found that this can lead to forgiveness. The focus to instill the idea of Create Value and Forgiveness is a life-changing combination and magnificent way to live life.

What is the concept of Create Value? The idea is that, whatever you face in life, you can find value in and use it as a place of strength. It can be a large mind shift to undertake, and the lifetime benefits of living with this ideal brings peace, achievement, honesty, excitement, fulfillment, and more.

The option of leaving pain in the past, unresolved and unhealed, are indeed available, but not healthy or fruitful for our current relationships. I believe you logically know this; however, over and over again, you turn to actions that hurt rather than help in life-long commitment. What is the answer? What are you to do? What I suggest here is that in order to make a better relationship today, you and I must create a better yesterday! Start with these points.

Acknowledge there is pain in your life (questions to ask yourself: What has caused you the most pain in life? What is your greatest fear?).

Work on forgiveness of the situation that caused your pain, remember that forgiveness is the releasing of a story that we were somehow unjustly hurt. Stop repeating the story in your mind, release it from silence, and understand that at times the past is not right, and release the energy of wanting a better past.

Create Value in your life from the pain the chapter expands on this idea.

Creating Value in your life is the call to action to stop allowing your past hurts and pain to run and ruin your life today. Just because something is in our past doesn't mean it is:

1. not still here; it is still alive inside you
2. that you can't influence it; you absolutely can

Search your past, find those painful memories and Create Value from them. This will bring more joy and happiness into your life today!

The simplest manner in which to present a new idea makes it more effective and digestible. That is why I developed the Create Value See-saw to present the states of :

**Pain** from the past, still unhealed

**Forgiveness** of past circumstances

**Create Value** in which life continues to improve
and goes up and up

This is the easiest way to visually express the idea of
Create Value:

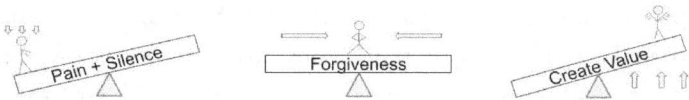

As long as you hold on to the pain in your life, it will
stay exactly where it has been and bring you down.
Forgiveness is the most powerful tool to bring balance
into your life and relieve the discomfort and issues of the
past pain that plays havoc in your life today. Only when
you Create Value in your life out of the past pain do you
take the memories and past feelings and transform them
into something that can bring you up and provide a positive in your life.

I love watching my two children on playgrounds. One
moment I hear pure screams of joy, the next screams of
pain. It occurred to me that in many ways, this is life, only
differing types of joys and pains. You likely do your very
best to live life experiencing higher highs (screams of
joy). Then there is a turn and life brings you challenge or
change (scream in pain). Up/Down Up/Down Up/Down,

like my children on the playground. How long can they stay up? How far down will they go?

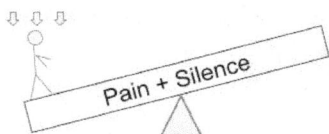

My children are very resilient, as children often are. They pick themselves up, brush off the dirt, cry some tears, and then go back to their play. They work to create joy (i.e. Create Value) on the playground all over again. However, adults do a variety of actions once pain enters: Stay Down, Blame, Relive the Moment, Suppress, Escape, pick ourselves up and ... suppress or escape from painful times. We've forgotten how to seek joy in the place of the occurred pain that we did as children. The challenging part, as adults, is that once pain is created, it is always there — impossible to unlearn. Especially with deep and/or early hurt, it infects your entire life. It doesn't take a break, it doesn't play fair, it is a constant and brings you down in all areas as it spreads.

There is a choice to work on forgiveness — a powerful tool. (Google.com gives you literally millions of books, articles and blogs to read on the topic). Forgiveness is not an automatic nor easy undertaking. It takes time plus work and it takes constantly living in forgiveness for the situation and with the other person and self. One of the challenges with forgiveness is: When is it complete? Is it ever complete?

When I was growing up, my parents continually pushed us in new directions and experiences. One of them was meditation, a difficult task for a teenager. I took classes and understood how to meditate and to learn the benefits for my mind and body. We went back to a refresher course a few months after I'd finished my training. My mom and I sat in a small room with 8 to 10 people while the instructor gave us pointers and refreshers. At one point the instructor asked the group:

"Who knows what happens after you have the stress in life under control and mastered aspects of meditation? What comes next?"

As any teenager, my mind was turning. I raised my hand. She called on me to answer, I think she was a bit surprised as I was the only teen and person who wanted to answer.

"You keep meditating, you never stop because there will always be more stresses in life." I said. You see, I thought it was a trick question and I was going to outsmart her.

That was not her correct answer.
"Um, yes, that is true, but you can also take our level 2 course."

I like my answer better, and today I apply it to forgiveness. When you think there is no more forgiveness to do in life, what do you do? First, congratulate yourself, acknowledge that there are layers of forgiveness, and be open to additional steps once the past resurfaces. Deep forgiveness of others and yourself is a multi-step process. With enough practice, it can become automatic in your life.

Ask someone you trust (and who really trusts you) about a specific painful memory that happened long ago. As they talk about it, watch their face. Has the pain completely left their life? The down-side of forgiveness is that the pain will come back in the strangest times and ways.

Back to our see-saw. We are not forced to stay in a state of pain forever because we have the option of forgiveness, as shown here.

Forgiveness gives you balance in life. Often we hear the phrase to forgive and forget — we know that is not possible. Logically, it's not advisable to forget a painful experience. That would only increase the likelihood of repetition. Our pasts offer us a powerful mechanism to learn so we can choose how we handle a similar painful experience.

It is possible to forgive, but it is not possible to purposefully forget. Think about a painful time in your past: the death of a loved one, you were mistreated, you broke the law, an intense fight, and so on. If you allow it, the pain will surface as will the emotion. Forgiveness does bring balance to life; it allows us to move along to our next positive experience.

Additionally, the experience brings an interesting awareness concerning the see-saw at the point of forgiveness — balance. At this point your past and future become more clear, there's a deeper understanding of key events. In this moment compassion is obtained, not only for others but also for self. Finally, an inner peace is obtained.

As with a see-saw and life, when things are in balance, it is often only for a short period of time. The breeze blows, someone shifts their weight, a memory reappears, the person who was gone forever is back. The see-saw falls back down to pain:

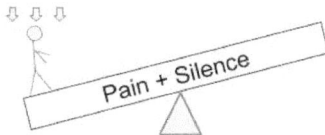

Nothing stays in perfect balance forever; life is about the challenges and changes it brings, not in standing still. Deep in thought, it occurred to me: **What comes after forgiveness? I further wondered... Is forgiveness ever**

**complete? If not, what can one do to move past the pain? Create Value** in life is the answer I searched for and that you also are searching for.

You must work to change the position of the see-saw into the position of Create Value. Only then will you have the ability to experience the joy of today without the pain from the past polluting it.

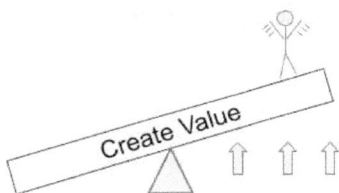

This book will lead you to recognize the key points in your life where forgiveness is needed and appropriate, in addition to the first steps of Create Value. The action of creation is up to you.

## YOUR FINAL STEP

Your final step, once you've strengthened your relationships and are committed to expanding your community, is to Create Value out of the past. The original question I pondered was: What comes after forgiveness?

I now understand the question isn't quite accurate. It is interesting but there is a deeper point which I missed at first. **It's not about what comes "after" but what complements forgiveness? The action that complements forgiveness is Create Value.** When you reflect on a past event, it can be experienced in a state of power, not pain. It is similar to the idea of writing more about a story — the next chapter or a new ending. It doesn't end in tears. No one can ever take a painful situation in their life, go back in time, and make it better. Create Value from the incident, move forward in life, and add to the story.

Over and over again, it is possible to literally re-live your pain (when you choose to not forgive or create value), dwelling on "what ifs." They replay in your head, and you try to understand what you did wrong, how horrible the other person was, or to beat yourself up. What are you really doing? You are re-examining the past to ensure that type of pain never enters life again.

More can be written, created, experienced, if you choose. Like my children on the playground, they fall. Do they decide to stay down and go home? No, most often they get back up and continue to write the story from that painful moment forward and are quickly back into the joy of life. Children know that if they stay down, that would not be fun. Adults fall and decide "never again will I fall down" and lose the opportunity to stand up again and have fun.

Will my child always have that fall in their memory? Yes, but there is a more powerful piece than the fall. When my child gets up and creates more fun, the fall loses its power.

As adults, when a fall happens and we stay down and allow the story to end, it concludes in pain. This pain influences the rest of your life. When you pick yourself up and create more out of the story, the fall loses its power and you create value in your life. The powerful story then influences you in a healthy manner for the rest of your life.

Back to our see-saw. We must look for ways to tip the see-saw into our favor.

In many ways it seems impossible/stupid to consider going back, in your mind, to that painful time. As stated earlier, many want to run and hide from the painful memory. The issue with the run and hide "solution" is that no matter how fast you run, the memory will keep up with you; you'll never be able to outrun it. The reason we have to go back is to Forgive (bring neutrality) and Create Value (bring power from pain).

Bring to mind one of the most painful memories in your life and consider where you are on the see-saw. Does the memory continue to bring you pain? How does the pain manifest? Have you started to forgive? Have you forgiven and brought some balance back to your life? The final question is: How have you created value from the painful experience? Only, in this final step, can the experience be a positive in your life and bring you more of what you value.

Consider one of my stories for a case of Create Value.

At age 33, I felt I had built the life I'd always wanted — the cars, living situation, relationship and finances. On top of this, I ate right and enjoyed exercising. It was a long build but life was continually getting better and looked to continue with more of the same. I'd recently taken a project working in a major Latin American city (a lifetime dream). I commuted weekly from the US, and while it was a challenge, I enjoyed the experience 100 percent.

I'd noticed an ache in my abdomen on one of

those flights south. I ignored it for a few days and it went away. A week later the discomfort returned and then faded. A few days later, the discomfort returned to my abdomen, and at this point I decided to see an urologist so that the doctor could tell me that everything was fine and to go back to life.

I set the appointment and kept it a secret from my wife, family and friends, telling myself that everything was fine, with no need to involve anyone else. I arrived for the appointment at 9:30 in the morning and entered to consult with the doctor. After hearing the information, the doctor stated that it was most likely of no concern and added that he'd like to do a physical exam and then sent me on my way.

You see, I had a lot to do as the project was entering its final two weeks and I was to get on a plane the next day to start to wrap it up. I had a million things going through my head. The doctor conducted a physical exam and sat back down in his stool, took some notes, and looked up to deliver the news. Yes, there was news to deliver. "You have cancer," the urologist stated. He continued, "You need to be on an operating table as soon as possible."

The doctor went on that this was a serious case, and he stated that he was going to get another urologist, so a second opinion could be rendered immediately. The second opinion was the same as the first.

I learned a valuable lesson that day, that no matter how great life is, how "right" you do things, life brings pain. My see-saw tilted into pain.

Pain entered my life big time. The life I'd built had hit full stop for an unspecified amount of time. The cars didn't matter. I stepped away from my work and projects, and finances were of little concern. My only focus was getting well and on my family.

My options, at that time, all appeared horrible — go to Latin America? Tell my family? Keep it to myself? I needed to speak to someone, get this secret off my chest, I needed a friend I could trust and who would give me excellent advice. As I walked back in the apartment, my wife walked out, off to university with a quick kiss. I called a good friend, A.W. In the middle of the work day, A.W. came right over after he received the call.

We spoke of options, decisions, and timing. I packed my bag to return to Latin America and finish the project that week. The next week, after speaking with my family about the situation, I was on an operating table on my way back to health — except I wasn't.

I received a round of encouraging tests, and the final step was to meet with an oncologist to obtain a clean bill of health. The oncologist, in a dry direct manner, told me that my cancer had spread and I needed to start chemotherapy the following Monday! To top it all off, A.W. decided to have a minor health issue checked after our meeting. During the evaluation, in an unfortunate turn of life, it was determined that he, too, had an aggressive form of cancer.

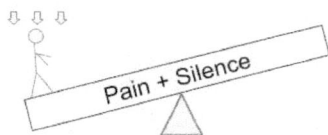

It was too difficult to comprehend for the two of us and our families. We supported each other and focused our energies on ourselves.

Two plus months of chemo passed slowly as I lost my hair and weight. A.W.'s health quickly deteriorated. When I received the news that the chemo was effective, I visited A.W. in the ICU to convey my news.

A.W. died a few weeks later.

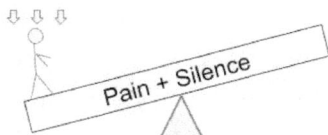

The physical healing process was slow, but I did make a full recovery. Mentally, it was more time consuming as it took time for the drugs to leave my system and to find stability. Non-stop I thought and searched for answers to this situation. As time passed things became easier and easier. I read and spoke with people I trusted, and after years of work, I still felt pain for the passing of my friend.

Years later, during one specific conversation, I wondered if there would ever be an opportunity to move past the loss. To find some closure, even today as I write and when I speak of A.W., I can feel the emotion and my voice quivers a bit. At this moment I discussed the friend-ship, the death, my work of forgiveness of loss, but that was not enough.

That was the moment of realization; the story was not over for me; no matter what I did it was a painful point in my life from years ago that was impacting me today. The story was not finished — there was more to be written.

My see-saw was vacillating between Pain and Forgive-ness, Pain and Forgiveness.

When I look back, there was no place for me to turn

for a positive. If I thought about an enjoyable time we had together, I quickly focused on the fact that there would never be another time similar in the future. The last memories I had were not soothing or enjoyable. Those were the ones stuck in my head.

At this point I concluded that I had to work on the aspect of Value Creation and continue writing the story of A.W. and my friendship with him. Where would the story go from here? It was up to me to write the story. No one else had answers; I had to create my own.

Many turn to others in life to tell them what to do in pain. **Here is the key — no one has your answers.** Only you have the answers about how to keep writing the story.

An incredible friend introduced me to an organization that raised money for cancer survivorship programs. I continued to write the story and went on a long bike ride. I rode for days with the group and celebrated the life of my friend and raised money for those dealing with cancer themselves. As I rode in A.W.'s name, the pain slipped away. I could feel the anger and pain shifting, and my focus altered to knowing that A.W. lived his life as he dreamed.

And the see-saw shifted from pain to value creation inside of me. I chose to focus my energy on the life A.W. led instead of his painful passing.

Pain + Silence    Forgiveness    Create Value

Would your loved ones want you to focus on the pain of their passing and leaving this world, or on their beautiful life? There is only one person accountable for the memory you hold onto — that is you reading this book. **No one can change the memory, except the memory holder.** If their passing is only seen as sadness, it will forever be a sad story in your memory and life. The important point is how you mentally hold the balance of their life's influence over your own. Choose a manner that tips the balance of their life to a positive and brings more to yours with create value.

We all have to deal with the death of loved ones, and most will deal with the cancer of someone close to us in life. However, more importantly, and on point, we all have to deal with pain in our lives where forgiveness is needed and important. This could be any number of reasons—relationship struggles, childhood pain, lost job, death of a loved one, parents' divorce, and any number of past experiences. Combine forgiveness with any or all of these and then involve Create Value and the door will open to pursuing your lifetime dreams.

Once the battle has been fought, what's the next step for those still here: in anger, loneliness, resentment, living in unforgiveness, or shutting out the world? None of these offer a life-time solution of more and positives.

Those who suffer the most, beyond yourself, are those who are here today with you and love you the most. Those who have passed are no longer battling and would want the fullest life for you, not to constantly look back in anguish. When people look back and find only grief, then as they continue in life, it will be filled with more heartache, and this pain will be a constant companion in life.

Maybe the pain you hold is not the passing of a loved member of your life. Take the story and make it your own, and keep writing your chapter until it ends on a high note. Releasing the pain from the past will allow you to move out of silence and interact fully with your communities. The sadness and loneliness of a history of pain and unforgiveness only leave you lonely.

# THEN THERE IS LOVE
## CONCLUSION

My conclusion, from working with thousands of individuals in personal growth, and years of research, is that your decisions to rely on silence in your relationships is the cause of your loneliness.

Loneliness is an issue in our society and the root of it (past pain, secrets and silence), in my opinion, will only grow and become more profound in the coming years. That position leads to more and more individuals feeling left out of society and community. One of the biggest hurdles to overcome loneliness is to break the self-confinement of silence. Self-imposed silence is often caused by the existence of secrets that have been carried too long and, over years, hidden in the darkest parts of who they are.

Your feelings of loneliness are created by your choice to be silent. In life and relationships, the main reason for choosing silence is the motivation to hold and hide your secrets.

Now is the time to take steps to create your community, break the silence, heal the pain, forgive and create value out of the past. I'm confident these steps will lead to your true community. **Only when you embrace community does community embrace you. Then there is love.**

The ultimate catch-22 in your *Life Unspoken*, in the secret-filled life, is you keeping secrets to protect yourself (and, you may believe, to protect others) and your relationship. While secrecy can accomplish this goal, there is a big price to pay. It ends up hurting you (in many ways) and the relationship suffers. The way out of past pain doesn't involve a black box buried deep in your consciousness.

Pain is a fascinating part of life; often it is very sharp at first and then fades. Although never completely fading away, over time we become accustomed to the dull discomfort, and it stays with us day after day after day... Here is a little story that my grandmother loved to tell about pain in life.

Two men, one a farmer the other a repair man, and a dog sit on a porch. The two men are carrying on conversation when the repairman is interrupted by a loud "YAP" from the dog. The farmer doesn't move a muscle, the repairman is startled. After the "yap" of pain, the dog closes its eyes and falls asleep once again.

The repair man almost believes he was imagining things and continues what he was saying. A few moments later, the dog lets out another "yap" and the repairman is sure the dog is in pain and is concerned for the animal.

He asks the farmer, "What is wrong with your dog?" The farmer responds that the dog is fine. The repairman laughs a bit and disagrees, "Why would the dog make such a sound if he was fine?"

The farmer looks at the dog and says, "He must be laying on that old rusty nail again."

The repairman thought; that makes perfect sense and no sense at all. He then follows up with another question. "Why would the dog stay on top of the nail if it is bringing him such pain?"

The farmer responds matter-a-factly, "Well, I guess the dog has not hurt enough to move off the nail."

The only thing that a memory of pain will bring you is more pain until it is turned into a place of strength. Have the difficulties in your life caused enough pain to influence you to move off the nail?

Your loved ones and your community are waiting for you with open arms; they want you to come home. They desire a relationship with the peaceful individual you once were and can be again. They want the true you to walk back into their life.

# YOUR REVIEW IS MUCH APPRECIATED

Please take a moment to **review this book**; you can do so on
Amazon and Goodreads - **Thank You!**

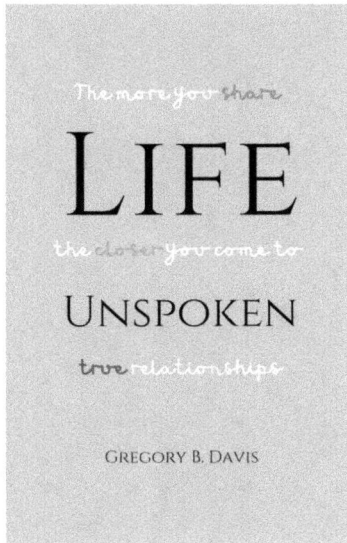

The more you share

# LIFE

the closer you come to

## UNSPOKEN

true relationships

GREGORY B. DAVIS

---

**Life Unspoken**

The more you share, the closer you come to true relationships

# THE BIGGEST GIFT OF ALL

Preview of my Upcoming Book

# THE BIGGEST GIFT OF ALL

## Introduction

My little boy watches me. It has been six years, and every day he watches me more intently than the day before. In fact, he has been watching me so closely that he has started mimicking my body movements and my wording. He also recognizes my mistakes now and brings them to my attention. I am the biggest contributor to his development as a little man and whether I like it or not, whether I'm 100% aware of it at all times or not my actions (mistakes and all) influence the way he sees me and has an effect on the person he becomes. We must never forget our main influence will take place during their earlier years of life. However it does not end there. Parents continue to be a source of reference.

For me, learning from my parents did not end when I became an adult. To this day, my parents play a big role in my life development in many ways. For example, I observe how they handle difficult situations and face challenges. From them, I learn about maintaining loving relationships, and their level of life excitement and desire to learn and achieve impacts me. I see how the choices they make affect their lives, and I am impacted by their ability to make healthy decisions. Importantly, I also see when my parents make mistakes. Just like my son sees them in me.

This book is about **you, your child and your relationship** - no matter what moment you are experiencing right now as a parent. I will take you on an introspection journey specifically designed to enhance your life, expand your child's horizons and **create a closer bond** between you two. The key wisdom in this book **begins with the adult caregiver,** and then it **ripples out to every part of your life.** In this continuous life-exchange cycle, where should you, the reader, and I, the author, start? We meet at parenthood.

First, we start the book with strategies for enhancing your life by **dismantling the comfort zone** that is holding you back from **facing your fears.** Before you can assist your child in facing their fears you must be clear about your own fears and understand what these fears cost you in your life. An important part of the journey toward a full personal life is to acknowledge that you are constantly moving towards love or staying stuck in fear (pursuit of love or avoidance of fear). We have a higher purpose as parents besides demonstrating a life of the daily grind. We are setting our children up for a lifetime of passion, joy and excitement. So, it is up to us, the parents, to choose healthy priorities, as these decisions impact our child's life forever.

Next, we will work on opening the doors for our children by observing their lives and offering guidance with **love and hope.** Childhood shapes life, it sets the foundation f o r e v e r. Another part of the introspective journey you will go on is to create space and time to think about activities and challenges you would like to face along with your child, having their welfare at heart. Working through challenges together, prepares your child to face challenges on their own in the future. In addition, modeling this process for your child helps them comprehend the beauty in pursuing one's dreams without fear. As they stretch out of their comfort-zone, they will have a powerful understanding of life and *prosper...* moving up and forward in their lives.

Finally, we will go over strengthening our relationship with our kids. As parents, this relationship may possibly be **our biggest and most glorious contribution to the world;** that is how we raised our children for their own lives and continually pass knowledge and wisdom to them. A closer bond truly can become **The Biggest Gift of All** —a life for them in which they bravely choose to pursue love, face their fears, and take control of their decisions, resulting in full and purposeful living.

My greatest wish for you with this book is that you realize that you are teaching your children as you experience growth, fulfillment and accomplishments. **As you enrich yourself, you are enriching them.** Take this book and this moment as an opportunity of a lifetime to expand your life, their horizons and the relationship between the two of you.

My little boy is watching me every moment. So, I

often wonder "what is he taking away from this moment?" I want him to live life with passion and joy, conquering life's goals while chasing his biggest dreams. Soon, it will all be up to him; but right here, right now it is entirely up to me. How he faces life... It is up to me.

I will **let love lead the way.**

**ALSO BY GREGORY B. DAVIS**

*Fight or Flight! Make better decisions to enjoy your life*

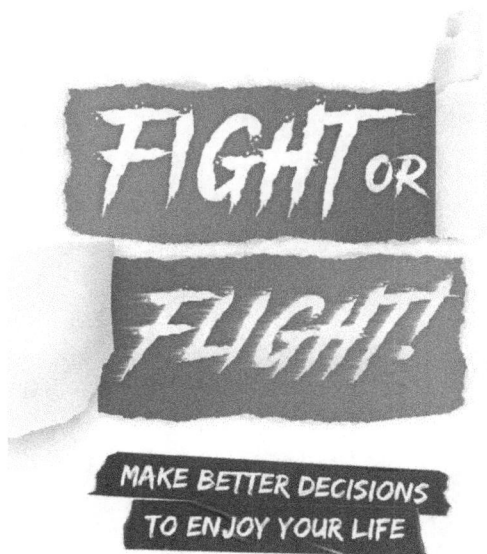

GREGORY B. DAVIS

# ALSO BY GREGORY B. DAVIS

*Wisdom is the Beginning - A better life starts with Knowledge*

LIFE INSIGHT FROM HISTORICAL EXPERTS

# WIS
# D_M

A better
life starts
with
knowledge

## IS THE BEGINNING

GREGORY B. DAVIS

# REFERENCE LIST

## Reading List

British Red Cross. (2016 December). "Trapped in a Bubble - An investigation into triggers for loneliness in the UK." www.redcross.org.uk/-/media/documents/about-us/research-publications/health-social-care-and-support/co-op-trapped-in-a-bubble-report.pdf?la=en&hash=5EFA679100B4EBCF0FEB705EB582E2775BD83844

Croteau, Jill. (2019, November 19). Global News. "Alberta documentary sheds light on men in the oilpatch and suicides". Globalnews.ca/news/6191176/alberta-docu-mentary-men-mental-health-oilpatch-suicides/

Mineo, Liz. (2017, April 11). The Harvard Gazette. "Good Genes are nice, but joy is better". News.harvard.e-du/gazette/story/2017/04/over-nearly-80-years-harvard-study-has-been-showing-how-to-live-a-healthy-and-happy-life/

Cacioppo, John, Fowler, James, Christakis, Nicholas. (2009). DASH Digital Access to Scholarship at Harvard.

Alone in the Crowd: "The Structure and Spread of Loneliness in a Large Social Network". Dash.harvard.edu/bitstream/handle/1/426347/christaki_alonecrowd.pdf?sequence=2

Wegner, Daniel M. (1994). American Psychological Association. "Ironic processes of mental control." www.redirectaniety.com/wp-content/uploads/2015/04/Wegner1994.pdf

Jaffe, Eric. (2006, July). Association for Psychological Science. "The Science Behind Secrets". www.psychologicalscience.org/observer/the-science-behind-secrets

**Video List**

Warren, Frank. (2012). Half a million secrets. TED2012. www.ted.com/talks/frank_warren_half_a_million_secrets?utm_score=sms&utm_medium=social&utm_campaign=tedspread

Guest Author. (2014). The art - and science - of sharing a secret. www.ideas.ted.com/the-art-and-science-of-sharing-a-secret/amp/

TEDx Talks. (2013, September 9). Cacioppo, John. "The Lethality of Loneliness: John Cacioppo at TEDxDesMoines". YouTube. Youtu.be/_ohxlo3JoAo

# END NOTES

## Loneliness

1. Cacioppo, John, Fowler, James, Christakis, Nicholas. (2009). DASH Digital Access to Scholarship at Harvard. Alone in the Crowd: "The Structure and Spread of Loneliness in a Large Social Network". https://1library.net/document/dy4d3gky-crowd-structure-spread-loneliness-large-social-network.html .
2. ibid.
3. UK Government. (2018, October 15). "PM launches Government's first loneliness strategy". www.gov.uk/government/news/pm-launches-governments-first-loneliness-strategy .
4. Ibid.
5. Schulze, Hannah. (2018, April 16). "Loneliness: An Epidemic?". http://sitn.hms.harvard.edu/flash/2018/loneliness-an-epidemic/ .
6. Statista. (date accessed 2020, June 30). "Percentage of single-person households, by state U.S. 2018". www.statista.com/statistics/242284/percentage-of-single-person-households-in-the-us-by-states/.
7. CBS News. (2018, May 3). "Many Americans are lonely, and Gen Z most of all, study finds". www.cbsnews.com/amp/news/many-americans-are-lonely-and-gen-z-most-of-all-study-finds/ .
8. ibid.
9. Polack, Ellie. (2018, May 1). Cigna. "New Cigna Study Reveals Loneliness at Epidemic Levels in America". www.cigna.com/newsroom/news-releases/2018/new-cigna-study-reveals-loneliness-at-epidemic-levels-in-america .
10. Sullivan, Kate. (2015, December). Women's Health. "All the Messed-Up Sh*t That Keeping Secrets Does to Your Body". www.womenshealthmag.com/life/a19941558/keeping-secrets-messes-up-body/.
11. DiJulio, Bianca; Hamel, Liz; Munana, Caily; Brodie, Mollyann. (2018, August 30). KFF.com. "Loneliness and Social Isolation in the US, the UK and Japan: An International Survey". www.kf-

f.org/report-section/loneliness-and-social-isolation-in-the-united-states-the-united-kingdom-and-japan-an-international-survey-introduction/ .

12. Anderer, John. (accessed 2020, July). Studyfinds.org. " Lockdown loneliness: COVID-19 quarantine has quarter of adults feeling like they have no friends." www.studyfinds.org/lockdown-loneli-ness-covid-19-quarantine-has-quarter-of-adults-feeling-like-they-have-no-friends/ .

13. Murthy, Vivek H., (2020, March 2) The Wall Street Journal. "Are You Lonely? You're Not Alone". www.wsj.com/amp/articles/are-you-lonely-youre-not-alone-11583174002

## The Study

1. Stossel, Scott. (2013, May). The Atlantic. "What Makes Us Happy, Revisited". www.theatlantic.com/amp/article/309287 .

2. Mineo, Liz. (2017, April 11). The Harvard Gazette. "Good Genes are nice, but joy is better". News.harvard.edu/gazette/sto-ry/2017/04/over-nearly-80-years-harvard-study-has-been-show-ing-how-to-live-a-healthy-and-happy-life/ .

3. Stossel, Scott. (2013, May). The Atlantic. "What Makes Us Happy, Revisited" www.theatlantic.com/amp/article/309287 .

## Silence is Violence

1. Young, Karen. (date accessed 2020, June 15). HeySigmund.com. "The Surprising Truth About The Silent Treatment." www.heysigmund.com/the-silent-treatment/.

2. Young, Karen. (date accessed 2020, June 15). HeySigmund.com. "The Surprising Truth About The Silent Treatment." www.heysigmund.com/the-silent-treatment/.

3. Young, Karen. (date accessed 2020, June 15). HeySigmund.com. "The Surprising Truth About The Silent Treatment." www.heysigmund.com/the-silent-treatment/.

## Push Love Away

1. Burdick, Alan. (2017, May 27). The New Yorker. "The Secret Life of Secrets". https://www.newyorker.com/tech/annals-of-technology/the-secret-life-of-secrets .
2. Winerman, Lea. (2011, October). American Psychological Association. "Suppressing the 'White Bears'" . www.apa.org/monitor/2011/10/unwanted-thoughts .

## When Silence equals Secrets

1. Merriam-Webster Dictionary. www.merriam-webster.com/dictionary/secret .
2. Petter, Olivia. (2017, October 2). Independent. "Keeping Secrets Harms Your Health and Your Career, Study Finds". https://www.independent.co.uk/life-style/keeping-secrets-harms-health-career-study-men-women-a7978076.html?amp.
3. Slepian, Michael. (2019, February 5). Scientificamerica.com "Why the Secrets You Keep Are Hurting You." www.scientificamerican.com/article/why-the-secrets-you-keep-are-hurting-you .
4. Crew, Bec. (2017, May 29). Science Alert. "Science Predicts You're Hiding 13 Secrets - And Nearly Half of Those You've Never Told a Soul". www.sciencealert.com/science-predicts-you-re-hiding-13-secrets-and-half-of-those-you-ve-never-told-a-soul .

## Layers of Secrets

1. Crew, Bec. (2017, May 29). Science Alert. "Science Predicts You're Hiding 13 Secrets - And Nearly Half of Those You've Never Told a Soul". www.sciencealert.com/science-predicts-you-re-hiding-13-secrets-and-half-of-those-you-ve-never-told-a-soul .
2. Slepian, Michael. (2019, July 1). Society for Personality and Social Psychology. "The Problem With Keeping A Secret." www.spsp.org/news-center/blog/slepian-keeping-secrets .
3. Luft, Joseph & Ingham, Harrington. (1955). Wikipedia. "Johari Window". www.wikipedia.org/wiki/johari_window .

## Your Secrets, Your Body

1. Fellizar, Kristine. (2019, June). Bustle.com. "7 Weird Things Your Body May Do When You Keep Secrets, According to Experts." https://www.bustle.com/p/7-weird-things-your-body-may-do-when-you-keep-secrets-according-to-experts-18000839.
2. Roberts-Grey, Gina. (2013, October). Forbes.com. "Keeping Secrets Can Be Hazardous To Your Health." www.Forbes.com/sites/nextavenue/2013/10/24/keeping-secrets-can-be-hazardous-to-your-health/amp/.
3. Belilovskaya, Liz. (2019, December). Brain World Magazine. "How Secrets Make Us Sick." www.brainworldmagazine.com/secrets-make-us-sick/amp/.

## Reasons to Break Silence

1. Slepian, Michael. (2019, February 5). Scientificamerican.com "Why the Secrets You Keep Are Hurting You." www.scientificamerican.com/article/why-the-secrets-you-keep-are-hurting-you.
2. Slepian, Michael. (2019, February 5). Scientificamerican.com "Why the Secrets You Keep Are Hurting You". www.scientificamerican.com/article/why-the-secrets-you-keep-are-hurting-you.
3. Slepian, Michael. (2019, July 1). Society for Personality and Social Psychology. "The Problem With Keeping A Secret." www.spsp.org/news-center/blog/slepian-keeping-secrets .
4. Warren, Frank. (2012). Half a million secrets. TED2012. www.ted.com/talks/frank_warren_half_a_million_secrets?utm_score=sms&utm_medium=social&utm_campaign=tedspread .

## Protective Silence

1. Slepian, Michael. (2019, February 5). Scientificamerica.com "Why the Secrets You Keep Are Hurting You." www.scientificamerican.com/article/why-the-secrets-you-keep-are-hurting-you .

2. Burdick, Alan. (2017, May 27). The New Yorker. "The Secret Life of Secrets". https://www.newyorker.com/tech/annals-of-technology/the-secret-life-of-secrets .

## Embrace Community

1. Dunn, Elizabeth. (2019, April 21). Exploring Your Mind "When Talking to Strangers Is Easier than Talking to People You Know". www.exploringyourmind.com/talking-to-strangers-easier-than-talking-to-people-you-know/amp/ .
2. Cherry, Kendra. (2019, December 9). Verywellmind.com "The Health Consequences of Loneliness". https://www.verywellmind.com/loneliness-causes-effects-and-treatments-2795749 .
3. Bradt, George. (2015, May 27). "Forbes: The Secret of Happiness Revealed by Harvard Study". https://www.forbes.com/sites/georgebradt/2015/05/27/the-secret-of-happiness-revealed-by-harvard-study/?sh=7d1d7e246786 .

## Motion Influences Emotion

1. Keltner, Dacher. (2010, September). Greater Good Magazine."Hands On Research. The Science of Touch". www.greatergood.berkeley.edu/article/item/hands_on_research .
2. Harvard Health Publishing. (2014, March). www.health.harvard.edu."Hugs heartfelt in more ways than one". www.health.harvard.edu/newsletter_article/
in_brief_hugs_heartfelt_in_more_ways_than_one .